BERTOLT BRECHT

Mother Courage and Her Children

Translated from the German by
JOHN WILLETT

With Commentary and Notes by
HUGH RORRISON

METHUEN DRAMA

Methuen Student Edition

15 17 19 20 18 16 14

This Methuen Student Edition first published in 1983
by Methuen London Ltd
by arrangement with Suhrkamp Verlag, Frankfurt am Main
This translation of *Mother Courage and Her Children* first published
in 1980 by Eyre Methuen Ltd
Translation copyright © 1980 by Stefan S. Brecht.
Original work entitled *Mutter Courage und ihre Kinder*
Copyright 1940 by Arvid England Teaterforlag, a.b.,
renewed June 1967 by Stefan S. Brecht
Copyright 1949 by Suhrkamp Verlag, Frankfurt am Main.
Commentary and Notes in this edition copyright © 1983 by
Methuen London Ltd

Methuen Publishing Ltd
215 Vauxhall Bridge Road, London SW1V 1EJ

A CIP catalogue record for this book is available from the British Library

ISBN 0 413 49270 2

Methuen Publishing Limited Reg. No. 3543167

Papers used by Methuen Publishing Limited
are natural, recyclable products made from wood grown in
sustainable forests. The manufacturing processes conform to
the environmental regulations of the country of origin

Printed and bound in Great Britain
by Cox & Wyman Ltd, Reading, Berkshire

Front cover photograph shows Helene Weigel as Courage
(Photo: Hainer Hill).

*Thanks are due to John Willet and to Herta Ramthun of the
Brecht Archive for help in the preparation of this edition*

Contents

Bertolt Brecht 1898-1956

Brecht's life falls into three distinct phases demarcated by his forced exile from his native Germany during the Hitler years. From 1898-1933 he is in Germany; from 1933-1947 he is in exile in various parts of the world; in 1947 he returns to Europe, first to Switzerland then to Berlin.

Germany

1898   Eugen Berthold Friedrich Brecht born on 10 February at Augsburg where his father was an employee and later director of the Haindl paper mill.

1908   Brecht goes to Augsburg Grammar School (Realgymnasium) where he is an indifferent pupil and a rebel in his quiet way, numbering among his friends Caspar Neher, later his designer. Brecht was almost expelled for taking a dismissive, anti-patriotic line when set an essay with the title 'It is a sweet and honourable thing to die for one's country'.

1917   Brecht enrols as a medical student at Munich University, where he also attends Arthur Kutscher's theatre seminar. He samples the bohemian literary life of the city.

1918   Brecht is conscripted and serves as a medical orderly, though he still lives at home. He writes *Baal*, a rumbustious, even outrageous dramatic tribute to natural drives and anarchic sexuality, and does theatre reviews for the local newspaper, *Augsburger Neueste Nachrichten*.

1919   Brecht writes *Drums in the Night*. He meets the comedian Karl Valentin, the theatre director Erich Engel, and actresses Blandine Ebinger, Carola Neher and Marianne Zoff.

1920   Brecht visits Berlin.

1921   Brecht's registration at Munich University is cancelled. An attempt to make himself known in literary circles in Berlin ends with him in hospital suffering from malnutrition. His new friendship with Arnolt Bronnen, the playwright, leads him to change the spelling of his name to Bertolt, or Bert.

1922   Brecht marries Marianne Zoff. He writes *In the Jungle of Cities*.

1923   Brecht's daughter Hanne is born. The activities of Hitler's National Socialists are hotly discussed in Brecht's Munich circle. The first productions of *In the Jungle of Cities* and *Baal* take place in Munich and Leipzig respectively.

1924   Brecht directs Christopher Marlowe's *Edward II* which he and Lion Feuchtwanger had adapted. He was already using certain devices (plot summaries before scenes, white face make-up to indicate fear) to induce critical detachment in actors and audience. He finally settles in Berlin and is taken on as dramaturg (literary adviser) at Max Reinhardt's Deutsches Theater. The actress Helen Weigel bears him a son, Stefan.

1926   *Man Equals Man* premiered at Darmstadt and Düsseldorf. He works on a play (which he never finished) called *Joe Fleischhacker*, which was to deal with the Chicago Wheat Exchange, leads him to the study of Marx as the only adequate method of analysing the workings of capitalism.

1927   Brecht divorces Marianne Zoff. He works with Erwin Piscator, the pioneer of communist political theatre in Germany, on a dramatisation of Hašek's novel *The Good Soldier Schweik*.

1928   *The Threepenny Opera*, music by Kurt Weill, words by Brecht (based on a translation of John Gay's *Beggar's Opera* by Brecht's friend and collaborator Elisabeth Hauptmann) opens at the Theater am Schiffbauerdamm and becomes the hit of the season. Brecht had provocatively transferred bourgeois manners to a Soho criminal setting.

1929   Brecht marries Helene Weigel. *The Baden-Baden Cantata* is staged at the Baden-Baden Music Festival, music by Hindemith.

1930   Brecht's daughter Barbara born. His *Lehrstück* or didactic play, *The Measures Taken*, is given its first performance in Berlin. The communist didactic plays for amateur performance were intended to clarify the ideas of the performers as much as the audience. The first performance of *The Rise and Fall of the City of Mahogonny*, an opera with words by Brecht and music by Kurt Weill causes a riot as the Nazis voice their criticism at Leipzig. In his notes on the opera Brecht tabulates the differences between the traditional *dramatic* (or Aristolelian) and the new *epic* (or non-Aristolelian) theatre at which he is aiming.

1931   Brecht completes *St Joan of the Stockyards*.

1932   Brecht's only film, *Kuhle Wampe,* is held up by the censor.
His dramatisation of Maxim Gorky's novel *The Mother* is
performed by a left-wing collective in Berlin, music by Eisler,
It demonstrates the development of a worker's mother
towards proletarian class-consciousness. Beginning of Brecht's
friendship with Margarete Steffin. Brecht studies Marxism
under the dissident communist Karl Korsch.

Exile

1933   The Nazis come to power. The night after the German
parliament building (the Reichstag) is burnt down, Brecht
flees with his family to Prague. He moves to Vienna, then
Zurich, finally settling on the island of Fyn in Denmark.
His friendship with Ruth Berlau begins.

1934   Brecht visits London. The themes of flight and exile enter
his poetry.

1935   Brecht is stripped of his German citizenship. He visits
Moscow and meets the Soviet dramatist Sergei Tretiakov.
He attends the International Writers' Conference in Paris.
He visits New York to look in on a production of *The
Mother,* which does not meet with his approval.

1936   Brecht attends the International Writers' Conference in
London. He writes anti-fascist poetry.

1937   Brecht attends the International Writers' Conference in
Paris.

1938   Brecht finishes writing *Life of Galileo*. *Fear and Misery of
the Third Reich* is given its first performance in Paris.

1939   Brecht moves to Stockholm with his family. He finishes
writing *Mother Courage and Her Children*.

1940   German forces march into Denmark. Brecht's household
moves to Helsinki in Finland where his friendship with the
writer Hella Wuolijoki begins.

1941   Brecht completes *Mr Puntila and His Man Matti, The Good
Person of Szechwan* and *The Resistable Rise of Arturo Ui*.
He writes war poetry and 'Finnish Epigrams'. Leaving
Finland Brecht travels through the Soviet Union via
Leningrad and Moscow (where Margaret Steffin dies) to
Vladivostock and sails to the U.S.A. He arrives in Los
Angeles in July and settles with his family in Santa Monica.
He makes contact with other exiles (Heinrich Mann,
Lion Feuchtwanger and Fritz Lang, the film director)

and with the natives (Orson Welles). First performance of *Mother Courage and Her Children* in neutral Switzerland.

1942   Brecht prepares his *Poems in Exile* for publication. He participates in the anti-war, anti-fascist activities of exile groups. He meets Charles Laughton.

1943   The first performances of *The Good Person of Szechwan* and of *Life of Galileo* take place in Zurich. Brecht writes *The Caucasian Chalk Circle*.

1944   Brecht becomes a member of the newly formed Council for a Democratic Germany. W.H. Auden works on an English version of *The Caucasian Chalk Circle*. Brecht studies Arthur Waley's translations of Chinese poetry.

1945   *Fear and Misery of the Third Reich* is given its first English performance in New York under the title *The Private Life of the Master Race*. Brecht and Charles Laughton complete an English version of *Life of Galileo*.

1946   The first performance of Brecht's adaptation of Webster's *The Duchess of Malfi* takes place in Boston.

1947   Charles Laughton appears in the title role of *Life of Galileo* in Beverly Hills and New York. Brecht appears before the *House Committee on Unamerican Activities* and proves himself a master of ambiguity when cross-examined about his communist sympathies.

Return

Brecht and Helene Weigel go to Zurich, leaving their son Stefan, who is an American citizen, in the U.S.A. Brecht applies for an Austrian passport. (Helene Weigel is Austrian.) He meets Max Frisch, his old friend and designer Caspar Neher, and the playwright Carl Zuckmayer.

1948   Brecht's adaptation of *Antigone of Sophocles* is performed in Chur, Switzerland, and *Mr Puntila and His Man Matti* is given its first performance in Zurich. He publishes the *Little Organum for the Theatre*. Brecht travels to Berlin and starts rehearsals of *Mother Courage* at the Deutsches Theater in the Soviet sector of the city.

1949   *Mother Courage* opens at the Deutsches Theater with Helene Weigel in the title role. Brecht visits Zurich again before settling in Berlin. The *Berliner Ensemble*, Brecht and Helene Weigel's own state-subsidised company, is formed and opens with *Puntila*.

1951   *The Mother* is performed by the *Berliner Ensemble*. Brecht

finishes the first version of his adaptation of Shakespeare's
Coriolanus.

1953   Brecht is elected President of the German section of the
       PEN Club, the international writers' association. On
       17 June there are strikes and demonstrations protesting
       about working conditions in the German Democratic
       Republic. Brecht writes a letter to the Secretary of the
       Socialist Unity Party which is released to the press in a
       doctored form.

1954   The Berliner Ensemble moves into its own home, the
       Theater am Schiffbauerdamm (where he had triumphed
       with *The Threepenny Opera* in 1928), and performs *The
       Caucasian Chalk Circle*. Brecht makes public his objections
       to the Paris Treaty (which incorporated the Federal
       Republic of Germany into Nato) and to re-armament in
       general. The Berliner Ensemble's productions of *Mother
       Courage* and Kleist's *The Broken Pitcher* are enthusiastically
       received as the highlights of the Paris Theatre des Nations
       festival. *Mother Courage* is awarded the prizes for best play
       and best production.

1956   Brecht is prepararing the Berliner Ensemble, which by that
       time has become generally recognised as the foremost
       progressive theatre in Europe, for a visit to London when
       he dies of a heart attack on 14 August. The visit went ahead
       and *Mother Courage, The Caucasian Chalk Circle,* and
       Trumpets and Drums were presented at the Palace Theatre
       at the end of August for a short season — a landmark in
       Brecht's reception in the United Kingdom.

Mother Courage's journey

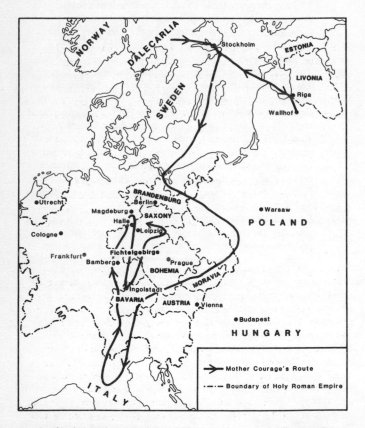

Europe in the 17th century. Not every scene in the play is geographically located. It opens in Dalecarlia, scene 2 is at Wallberg, scene 3 in Poland, between scenes 4 and 5 Courage traverses Poland, Moravia, Bavaria, Italy, and returns through Bavaria to Magdeburg for scene 5. Scene 6 is at Ingolstadt, scene 9 in the Fichtelgebirge and scenes 10 and 11 near Halle.

Plot

Mother Courage is a canteen-woman serving with the Swedish
Army during the Thirty Years War (1618-48). Despite an early
warning that war can never be all take and no give she intends to
make a living off the war while keeping her children out of it, but
her brave son Eilif is tempted into the infantry, kills a peasant
too many and is executed by his own side. Her honest son Swiss
Cheese defends the regimental cashbox too conscientiously when
he is captured and is executed by the enemy. Mother Courage
changes sides twice as she criss-crosses Europe, accompanied first
by the hypocritical Chaplin, then by the womanizing cook, and
her business first prospers, then declines. Her warm-hearted
daughter Kattrin dies warning the sleeping town of Halle that the
enemy is at the gates. Bowed and alone, Mother Courage drags her
battered waggon off seeking business as usual. Her tribulations have
taught her nothing.

Scene 1
1624, in Sweden. During a truce in the Swedish-Polish War a
recruiter and his sergeant who have been trying without success to
enlist new troops in Dalecarlia (see map) complain about the lack
of organisation and martial ardour in this peaceful and prosperous
province of Sweden. Mother Courage's waggon is drawn on by her
two strapping sons who catch the recruiter's professional eye.
Courage is a sutler, or canteen-woman, with the Second Finnish
Regiment (Finland is part of Sweden at this time). She sings verses
1 and 2 of 'Courage's Song'. She refuses to be intimidated when
asked for her papers, and when her brave son Eilif seems tempted
to follow the soldiers she tells the recruiter's fortune and prophesies
his early death. To put the fear of war into Eilif, Swiss Cheese and
Kattrin she draws black crosses signifying death out of the hat for
them too. She is back on her waggon and about to move when the
sergeant offers to buy a silver buckle and while she is making the
sale the recruiter takes Eilif off. The sergeant comments that you
cannot take from the war and not give.

Scene 2

1626, in Poland where the Swedes are besieging the Polish fortress
of Wallhof. Outside the General's tent Courage is haggling with his
cook over the price of a capon. She hears Eilif being congratulated
inside the tent for outwitting, robbing and killing some peasants
in the cause of 'true religion'. The cook now has to have food for
the new guest and Courage can and does charge him an outrageous
price for the bird. She remarks that only bad generals need heroic
soldiers. Eilif sings the jaunty 'Ballad of the Girl and the Soldier'
and dances a sword-dance. Courage adds a final verse in which the
foolhardy soldier dies in an icy river. Eilif is reunited with his
mother who cuffs him for risking his neck, while the Chaplain and
the General smile indulgently.

Scene 3

1629, in Poland. Courage beats down the price of black market
ammunition, observing that the armourer who is selling it is leaving
his own men defenceless. Swiss Cheese, whom she considers too
stupid to think of stealing and too honest anyway if he did think
of it had been made regimental paymaster. The war is looking up
and Courage's business prospects seem good. Yvette, the regimental
prostitute, throws aside her hat and red boots and bemoans the
downturn in her business now that it is known that she has VD.
She sings the 'Song of Fraternisation'. Courage tells Kattrin to let
Yvette's fate be a warning to her to have nothing to do with
soldiers. Courage grudgingly gives the Chaplain money for Eilif,
and the cook observes that it is best to be generous because
tomorrow Eilif could be dead. The Chaplain comments that it
would be a blessing to die in a holy war, but the cook dismisses this
ironically and Mother Courage concludes the discussion of the
motives of the men at the top by observing that they are in the war
for profit, just as she is. Meanwhile, unobserved, Kattrin tries on
Yvette's hat and boots and imitates her walk. This peaceful idyll
is interrupted as the Imperial forces overrun the camp. The cook
rejoins the General, the Chaplain hides his clerical garb, Yvette,
with fresh custom in prospect, powders her face and looks for her
boots. Courage smears Kattrin's face with ashes. Swiss Cheese runs
on clutching his cashbox and Courage tells him to throw it away.
She hauls down the Finnish regimental flag.

Three days later, Courage has survived interrogation. She is to
be allowed to carry on her business in the Imperial camp, and goes
off to fetch new supplies and an appropriate flag. When she comes
back, Swiss Cheese has been spotted after hiding the cashbox and

arrested. Yvette now has a rich old man in tow and Courage offers
to sell her the cart in order to raise money to save Swiss Cheese.
She haggles too long over the ransom and he is shot. Suspecting a
connection with Courage, the Imperial troops show her her son's
body, but she betrays no sign of recognition.

Scene 4
Still 1629. Mother Courage waits ouside the colonel's tent to
complain about damage to her cart. A young soldier storms in
intending to complain to the colonel that he has been cheated out
of his reward for saving the colonel's horse. Courage sings the 'Song
of the Great Capitulation' to show him that letting off steam in
front of your superiors is futile; the soldier abandons his protest.
Courage has also persuaded herself that in business discretion is the
better part of valour and she too lets the matter rest.

Scene 5
1631 in Saxony. In a ravaged village near Leipzig the Chaplain
rescues a peasant family from the ruins of their farm. Courage
refuses to hand over her shirts and the Chaplain moves her aside
bodily and tears up four shirts for bandages. Courage comments
that all she gets from victory is losses. Kattrin rescues a baby from
a burning house. A soldier tries to steal liquor. Courage relieves him
of a looted fur coat in lieu of payment.

Scene 6
1632, outside Magdeburg. As Courage takes stock and serves
soldiers who are dodging the funeral of Tilly, the Imperial General,
she discusses the fates of great men who strive for immortality only
to be frustrated when the lower ranks step out for a drink at the
crucial moment. Courage is concerned that the war might end, but
the Chaplain assures her that there will always be plenty of heroes
to replace dead generals. Courage is persuaded that the war will go
on and decides to buy in supplies. Kattrin, dismayed that the
marriage she has been promised after the war will never happen,
dashes off but her mother fetches her back and sends her into
Magdeburg to fetch stores. The Chaplain admires Courage's
dedication to her business and Courage observes that the way
things are ordinary folk have to have guts just to face the next day.
The Chaplain, as he clumsily chops wood for her, explains that his
real forte is sweeping people off their feet with sermons. He
suggests that perhaps a closer relationship is indicated since they
get on so well together, but Courage replies that she has no time

for personal affairs, her only aim being to bring her children and
her cart through the war safely. Kattrin returns, bleeding from a
wound above one eye but still clutching her bundles of supplies.
She creeps off, rejecting Yvette's red boots which her mother
offers as consolation. Courage remarks that, with a scar on her face
as well as her dumbness (she has not spoken since a soldier
molested her as a child), there is scant hope of finding a husband
for her after the war. A salute is fired over Tilly's grave, and
Courage remarks that at the moment her daughter's disfigurement,
and not Tilly's death, is the historical event that matters.

Scene 7
Still 1632. Mother Courage, with her cart well-stocked and a silver
necklace round her neck, has regained her confidence in the war.
Her career is at its peak. She celebrates with verse 3 of 'Courage's
Song'; war is nothing other than business, trading in blood instead
of boots.

Scene 8
Still 1632, in Saxony. An old lady and her son are trying to sell
their bedding to Courage to pay their taxes when the bells ring out
announcing peace. The cook returns and supplants the Chaplain
in Courage's favour. The Chaplain puts on his clerical garb again and
Courage tells him sarcastically that his war has turned out to be a
flop, provoking the Chaplain into calling her a hyena of the
battlefield, who cannot accept peace because she makes money out
of war. Whosoever sups with the devil needs a long spoon, he tells
her. This is too much for Courage, who sends the Chaplain packing.
On the cook's advice she decides to sell out before the bottom falls
out of the market. Yvette, now a rich colonel's widow, arrives and
identifies the cook as Puffing Pete, the womanizer who was her
original downfall. Courage goes to town to sell off her goods and
Eilif is led on under arrest. He has repeated his heroics of Scene 2,
robbing a peasant and killing his wife, but now it is peacetime and
the penalty is death. When Courage returns, the cook merely tells
her that Eilif dropped in after repeating one of his deeds of valour,
but had to go. Courage reports that war has broken out again and
invites the cook to join her. She sings verse 4 of Courage's Song as
they move off to rejoin her 'own side', the Swedes again.

Scene 9
1634, in Saxony. In a wintry landscape in the Fichtel Mountains.
Courage and the cook are begging outside a war-damaged parsonage
The cook has had a letter telling him he has inherited the family

inn at Utrecht. He invites Courage to run it with him, but when Courage puts the offer to Kattrin, he makes it clear that the business is too small to support three. He sings the 'Song of Solomon', on the theme of the futility of virtue. A voice from the manse offers them soup, and Kattrin, left outside, symbolically drapes a skirt of her mother's beside the cook's trousers on the cart-wheel. She is on the point of running away when her mother brings out some soup and tells Kattrin she has rejected the cook's offer, not, she hastens to add, because of her daughter but because she can't let the waggon go. The cook emerges to find them gone and his clothes in a heap on the ground.

Scene 10
Still 1634. Courage and Kattrin pause from pulling the waggon outside a house from which the 'Song of Home', on the theme of comfort and security, can be heard.

Scene 11
1636, in Saxony. On a farm outside Halle which is held by the Swedish forces, Imperial troops force the farmer's son to lead them into the sleeping town, first threatening his life and, when that fails, threatening to kill the family cattle. When they have gone the farmer's wife laments the fate of the sleeping citizens, among them her brother-in-law and his four children. At this, Kattrin climbs on to the roof with a drum to rouse the defenders. The soldiers return, fail to persuade her to stop drumming and shoot her. As her body rolls off the roof, the bells of Halle ring out the alarm.

Scene 12
The same day. Courage, unable to grasp that Kattrin is dead, sings her a lullaby. The peasants disabuse her and she tells them that they should not have mentioned the children. The peasant replies that she should have been with Kattrin when the soldiers came, not in town trying to get her cut. Courage pays them to bury Kattrin and hauls the cart off alone to catch up with business. The final verse of Courage's Song is heard offstage, ending with the lines:

Wherever life has not died out,
It staggers to its feet again.

Helene Weigel as Mother Courage in Brecht's own production for the Berliner Ensemble. *Photo: Hainer Hill*

Commentary

Meaning

What is a performance of Mother Courage and Her Children *primarily meant to show?*
That in wartime the big profits are not made by little people.
That war, which is a continuation of business by other means,
makes the human virtues fatal even to their possessors. That no
sacrifice is too great for the struggle against war.

(Brecht)

Brecht wrote the first complete version of *Mother Courage and Her
Children* in the years 1939 and 1940, but the play was conceived
earlier in his exile in Scandinavia before the outbreak of the
Second World War, as a warning to the Danes that they could not
hope to sit on the sidelines and profit with impunity if their
aggressive neighbour, Nazi Germany, went to war. Recalling his
initial purpose Brecht later commented,

> I wrote the play quite expressly for Scandinavia . . . What I had
> in mind in writing it was that the playwright's play might be
> staged in a few major cities, with its warning that you need a
> long spoon to sup with the devil . . . Nothing came of the
> projected productions. Writers can't write as fast as governments
> can whip up wars.

Mother Courage was not Brecht's first treatment of this theme. In
1927 he had collaborated on the dramatisation of Jaroslav Hašek's
novel *The Adventures of the Good Soldier Schweik* which
presented a satirical view of the Austrian army in the Great War
(1914-1918). This was staged at Erwin Piscator's communist
theatre in Berlin as part of a season of political plays which
consistently presented the Great War as a product of the capitalist
system. The link between war and capitalism was hammered home
in many obvious ways. In Piscator's production of *Rasputin, the
Romanovs, the War and the People which Rose Against Them,* for
example, there was a scene in which a British, a French, and a
German tycoon successively declaimed his patriotic faith in his

country's cause while projections of the belching chimneys of their arms factories on a screen behind them revealed the real interest in the war which they had in common. Brecht's treatment of the anti-war theme shares Piscator's assumption that all wars are capitalist ventures but the form he uses is subtler. He forgoes the immediacy of a subject from recent experience and sets his play in the remote seventeenth century. His play is intended not only to show a connection between war and capitalism, but also to demonstrate how the little man, or in this case the little woman, may contribute to wars in the vain hope of sharing the spoils. Mother Courage's canteen-waggon is a small business trying to profit from the war. Brecht invites us to consider the consequences of this, bearing in mind that her business interests prove to be incompatible with her second avowed concern which is to bring her three children safely through the conflict. By the twelfth scene she has lost them all, and yet at the end she still trudges off doggedly in search of the action. She has learnt nothing, Have we, her audience?

History

In selecting his subject Brecht passed over the destruction and carnage of the 1914-18 War, which was still relatively fresh in people's memories as he wrote and set the play in The Thirty Years War, which until the twentieth century had been the most destructive conflict fought on German soil. His selection of a remote hstorical period is part of a move away from the propagandistic directness of Piscator, and of Brecht's own communist didactic pieces (*Lehrstücke*) from the early thirties such as *The Measures Taken*, towards a cooler, more detached presentation of Marxist political ideas on the stage — a method of presentation Brecht called 'epic theatre'.

The Thirty Years' War (1618-1648) was part of the political upheaval that followed the Reformation which had divided Christian Europe into Protestant and Catholic states. In the play the Swedes stand for Protestantism (the Second Finnish Regiment being part of the Swedish Army), and the Imperial forces represent Catholicism, though it should be stressed at the outset that Brecht presents the religious conflict as a mere pretext for the war and insists that the underlying motive of the war leaders is profit.

The decisive phase in this struggle was fought out in the territories of the Holy Roman Empire (see map), a loose organization of substantially independent states which owed allegiance to the Holy Roman Emperor who was at this time

Emperor Ferdinand II, the ruler of Austria in Vienna.

The war began when the Protestant magnates of Bohemia and Moravia installed the Protestant Elector Palatine as their King in 1618. Bohemia and Moravia border on Austria, so the Catholic Ferdinand II intervened with the aid of troops and financial backing from Spain, the German Catholic states and the Papacy, defeated the Bohemian and Moravian forces and imposed Catholicism on their lands. Encouraged by this success the Emperor then tried to reduce the power of the Protestant princes in north Germany, and by 1629 was pressing them so hard that they called upon the King of Sweden, Gustavus Adolphus, to save the cause of Protestantism.

It is worth noting that the first scene of *Mother Courage* takes place in 1624 during the Polish-Swedish War which was separate from the Thirty Years War. Gustavus Adolphus had invaded Poland in 1621 to put an end to Polish claims to the Swedish throne and to establish Sweden's dominance round the Baltic. The war lasted until 1629, with a truce from 1622 to 1625, during which the play opens. It was characterized by the same mixture of religious, dynastic and political motives as the Thirty Years War proper, which by 1629 was involving Gustavus Adolphus too, as Mother Courage indicates in scene 3 when she remarks that,

> He set out by just trying to protect Poland against bad people, particularly the emperor, then it started to become a habit till he ended up protecting the whole of Germany. (p.27)

If one looks at the internal chronology of the play one finds that Mother Courage was initially far from being a *victim* of the Thirty Years War. Her children have been born as she followed the soldiers on the highways of Europe and the youngest, Kattrin, is twenty-five in scene 3. Her wagon has a signboard reading 'Second Finnish Regiment'. It flies the regimental flag which she hauls down when the Imperial forces attack (scene 3) with the remark that she never notices it since it has been there 25 years. This means that Mother Courage had left her native south Germany and gone to Scandinavia for the Swedish-Danish War by 1604, seven years before Gustavus Adolphus came to the throne, and fourteen years before the beginning of the Thirty Years War. All this gives added piquancy to her remark to the sergeant in scene 1 that she couldn't wait till war chose to come to Bamberg (p.7).

Gustavus Adolphus's victory at Wallhof in 1626, which provides the background to scene 2, completed his conquest of the Baltic

province of Livonia. At the same time further south, the Imperial
army under the generalship of Tilly and Wallenstein defeated the
Protestants under Mansfeld, the general who could not pay his
mercenary army, and therefore established the practice of living off
the countryside by systematically plundering the rural population,
just as Eilif learns to do when he joins the army.

After the defeat of Mansfeld, there was a lull in hostilities
during which Wallenstein was dismissed (1629), and it was only in
1631 when Saxony came in on the Protestant side that Gustavus
Adolphus turned the tide of the war by routing the Imperial forces
at Breitenfeld and again the next year at Rain am Lech, where Tilly
sustained wounds from which he died later at Ingolstadt. His
funeral provides the background to scene 6. Wallenstein was
recalled to lead the Imperial forces, but was defeated by Gustavus
Adolphus at Lützen near Leipzig, where the Swedish King was
killed (as Brecht tells us in the caption to scene 8). Two years later
the Swedish army sustained a defeat at Nördlingen (1634) which
marked its end as a major force in the war, which, however,
continued to rage sporadically on German soil until the Peace of
Westphalia (1648) resolved the political, religious and territorial
issues for a century.

Mother Courage, as has been shown, starts out in the Swedish
wars and only becomes involved in the Thirty Years' War in 1629
when Gustavus Adolphus is brought in. In that year she is captured
by Imperial troops. They have no regimental canteen-women, so
she is able to work for them in her old capacity as free-lance
supplier of food, drink, clothing, footwear and anything else she
can buy cheap and sell at a profit, such as pilfered ammunition in
scene 3, or the starving and destitute old lady's bedding in scene 8.
She is the regiment's unofficial canteen, bar and stores. In the two
years that follow her capture, Brecht tells us, she is ceaselessly on
the move across Poland, Moravia, Bavaria, Italy, Bavaria again and
back to Saxony. The death of Gustavus Adolphus in 1632 brings a
temporary peace and enables Mother Courage to change back to
the Swedish side. When we see her in scene 11, it is 1636 and she is
doing business in the Protestant town of Halle when Imperial
troops advancing on that city kill her daughter. Mother Courage is
equally prepared to do business with either side, and in this she
exemplifies the ideology which Brecht wishes us to see as dominant
in the Thirty Years War. War is just business, but with blood (or
lead in the original German) instead of boots.

The historical background is essential to a full understanding of the play as the subtitle, 'A Chronicle of the Thirty Years War' indicates, and Brecht explains elsewhere that 'chronicle' in this context means the same as 'history' as applied to Elizabethan plays, for example when we divide Shakespeare's works into tragedies, comedies and histories. However, one has to go no further than the titles of Shakespeare's histories to realise that Brecht is approaching his subject from a different angle. Shakespeare writes *Henry VIII*, or *Richard III*, or *Henry V*. He focuses on kings and examines the affairs of state, the interplay of politics and the personal motives of the men who control the destiny of nations. Brecht's chronicle on the other hand shows us none of the war leaders. King Gustavus Adolphus of Sweden is only named once, in the caption to scene 8, though his involvement in the war is discussed by Mother Courage, the Chaplain and the cook in scene 3. Of the Catholic leaders Count Johann Tilly is only mentioned in scene 6 when his funeral takes place offstage, and the enigmatic Wallenstein, Duke of Friedland, who for many, including the German dramatist Schiller, was the outstanding figure of the period is not mentioned at all. The reason for this is that Brecht is not interested in how they run the war, but in how their war affects people at the bottom of the social scale, so he has chosen as his heroine a woman who shares the profit-motive of the top men and will try to exploit anybody she meets. The plot is a series of business transactions, as if life consisted of nothing else, and we see soldiers reduced to pilfering their own stores, and raping, murdering and robbing the peasantry, we see peasants selling their last possessions, valuing their cattle more highly than their lives, having their farms bombarded by armies which don't bother to establish whose side they are on. *Mother Courage* is a chronicle of common life in the Thirty Years War, not life up at HQ. In all this the only figure who, financially speaking, comes out on top is the prostitute Yvette, and she ages from an attractive girl to a bloated hag in the process; the only figure who emerges with any moral credit is Kattrin.

Mother Courage

The character of Mother Courage has been subject to conflicting interpretations ever since the play was first performed in Zurich in 1941. Are we detached and critical as she makes her last exit, or are our emotions engaged as were those of Tennessee Williams who called the final moment of *Mother Courage* one of the most inspiring in all theatre, inspiring because of the woman's indomitability? Therese Giehse, who created the role in Zurich, gave a performance which Brecht acknowledged to have been extraordinary; but it was a performance which moved the critic Bernhard Diebold to write, 'she stood with her great mother's heart outside the confines of history, indeed in eternity'. This positive reception of a figure whom he himself saw as being misguided and refusing stubbornly to learn from experience moved Brecht to retouch his characterisation when he came to direct the first performance on German soil at Berlin in 1949. He was always willing to revise his plays if they did not work to his satisfaction in performance, which happened not infrequently. His figures were intended to have their own 'gestus', as he put it, that is to have a particular manner of speaking, moving and behaving which enabled the audience to assess their social value accurately. This was of course a task that the actor shared with the playwright. It was no comfort to Brecht that the Zurich critics who saw in Mother Courage 'the heart-rending vitality of all mother creatures' and called her 'Niobe-like' (Niobe being the archetype of suffering motherhood in Greek mythology, who turned herself to stone after the gods had killed her fourteen children) might be responding to the rich complexity and the contradictions of her character, so his revision set out to demonstrate more clearly than ever that Mother Courage's sense of motherhood is vitiated by her commercial instincts.

In the original version of scene 1 Eilif had gone off with the Recruiter while his mother was consoling the Sergeant with a swig of brandy. In the final version the Recruiter tells the Sergeant to 'involve her in a deal', and Mother Courage is tempted off the driving seat and round the back of her waggon with the prospect of a sale, and only then does the Recruiter persuade Eilif to go with him. The subordination of the maternal to the commercial is thus quite explicit. In scene 5 Mother Courage originally ripped up her shirts for bandages voluntarily, whereas in our version she has to be lifted aside bodily by the Chaplain so that *he* can get at the shirts. So here her concern that her daughter should not rush into the burning cottage is not matched by enough concern for the victims of the attack even to make her hand over a couple of shirts, whereas her daughter Kattrin is prepared to put her life at risk to save somebody else's baby. In scene 7 which follows her bitter realisation, prompted by the attack on Kattrin, that the war is 'a nice way to make a living', new lines and a new song were inserted to make her revived enthusiasm for the war more crass. In the final

scene some details were altered to bring out the hostility of the
peasants and so cool the scene's emotional impact; when she came
to pay the peasants to bury Kattrin, Helene Weigel, Brecht's wife,
who was playing the title role in Berlin, took out all her money and
then pointedly put one coin back in her bag before handing over
the rest, to show that even in this extremity the hard-bitten
business-woman in Mother Courage was not extinguished.

Brecht presents Mother Courage as a small-time war-profiteer.
She stands in Marxist terms for the *petite bourgeoisie,* the small
traders and white collar workers who stand a point higher on the
social scale than the proletariat and identify with the interests of
the ruling classes. She recognises that the men at the top are in the
war 'for what they can get'; she shares this profit-motive, but she
also realises that their fortunes and hers do not necessarily
coincide. A victory for the generals can lead to losses for her, and a
defeat to profits, as she tells the Chaplain in scene 3; indeed she
feels that political stalemate usually offers the best trading
conditions. Her shrewd practical reading of the situation does not
amount to historical insight, nor could Brecht have made her a
lucid analyst of her own situation without being anachronistic and
psychologically unconvincing. At only one stage in the play does
she have a glimmering of the truth of her situation and that is at
the end of scene 6 when she pronounces that the disfigurement of
her daughter is for her a more historic event than the death of the
Imperial General, Tilly. In Brechtian terms it is here she comes
closest to realising where her true interests lie, and she curses the
war. But the moment passes, business flourishes, and her first
words in the following scene are, 'I won't have you folk spoiling
my war for me!' Though *she* has forgotten the previous episode,
the audience sees the despondent Chaplain and the disconsolate,
still bandaged Kattrin trudging along beside her, walking reminders
of what war does to people, her people. In his 'Model-book' for the
1949 production Brecht recollects that after about 40 performances
they decided that Mother Courage should wear rings on her fingers
and a chain of silver talers round her neck at this stage. He says,

> Here, where she retracts her condemnation of the war, the signs
> of affluence, recently acquired, show, quite appropriately, that
> she has been bribed.

Brecht equates business profits with bribery.

A casual reading of the play might suggest that this is where our
opinion of Mother Courage is lowest, since this is where the cost to

others of her affluence is clearest. She has allowed Swiss Cheese to be executed, Kattrin to be molested, and still. . . . By scene 9 she and her business are going downhill against a background of increasing devastation and desolation. Brecht however indicates that she reaches her lowest point in scene 4.

> In no other scene is Courage so depraved as in this one, where she instructs the young man in capitulation to the higher-ups and then puts her own teaching into effect. Nevertheless Weigel's face in this scene shows a glimmer of wisdom and even nobility, and this is good. Because the depravity is not so much that of her person as that of her class, and because she herself at least rises somewhat above it by showing that she understands this weakness, and that it even makes her angry.

What makes it so depraved for Mother Courage to dissuade a raw recruit from sticking his neck out? The answer to this question leads us into the wider social implications of the parable that Brecht is telling. Individual protest is the engine of social change, and harnessed by a political organisation it acquires the force of revolution. In diverting the Young Soldier from his purpose Courage in a sense smothers his contribution to the class struggle. This is the social problem which fascinates Brecht in this scene which at first glance may not seem to relate to the story he has been telling up to now. The only other figure who raises the voice of protest is Kattrin (and she of course has to use a drum to make herself heard) as she demonstrates in her small way that an individual stand need not be futile.

Having said this, of course, one has only touched on one aspect of Brecht's comment above. In acting the scene of the Grand Capitulation Helene Weigel managed to give the impression that Mother Courage was aware of her own depravity, which Brecht suggests is a product of her class, more precisely of class conditioning. This means she could be changed by altered circumstances, although no such change takes place in the play. It is however one of Brecht's fundamental concepts that society makes men what they are, so that social change can alter them, and for the better. His plays were intended to lead his audience to the right conclusions about the social changes required.

Are Brecht's efforts to prevent the audience from sympathising with Courage successful? It is a measure of the complexity of the figure that it is impossible to be certain. Much depends on the actress playing the part. Courage is a repository of experience and folk-wisdom. She survives in a man's world because of her sense of humour, her shrewdness, her common-sense and her instinct for self-preservation. Her children perish because they have not inherited these traits, and not just because their mother is away, or has her mind on other things at the time. Kattrin is after all 32 when she decides to save Halle in scene 11. Courage sees through the system, and tries to play it, and that is where she fails. She does all she can but it is not enough. She is not the 'hyaena of the battlefield' the Chaplain accuses her of being, but she is partly that, and she leaves us with mixed feelings. She shares a pawky individualism and shrewd insight with another Brecht figure, Schweik in *Schweik in the Second World War*, but Schweik is a natural subversive, and in Nazism he has a more clear-cut antagonist, so there is never any doubt whose side we are on. *Mother Courage and her Children* is a more general parable, and it is richer for its ambiguity.

The children

Eilif is a tearaway. Left to himself he would have been a soldier long ago, so it is really his mother's doing that he is still available for the Recruiter to trick into the army in scene 1. He prospers in uniform, cutting down peasants with a will until he finally becomes the victim of his own aggression. Yet he has no regrets when he talks to the cook in scene 8, and as he leaves he says, 'Tell her it wasn't any different, tell her it was the same thing.' The virtue by which he perishes, his bravery, is a dubious quality, since it is mainly employed in harassing the civilian population.

Swiss Cheese is protected by his mother as long as possible, and when he has to join the army, she sees to it that it is in a non-combatant role as paymaster, where his guileless honesty will stand him in good stead. The trouble is that he does not have enough sense to know where to draw the line, and, rather than the honesty which is his virtue, it is his stupidity which causes his execution.

Kattrin should be played as intelligent from the start. She sees the mistakes people around her make — Swiss Cheese not noticing the Man with the Patch, Courage haggling over Swiss Cheese's ransom, or refusing to give up the shirts in scene 5 — but her dumbness prevents her from intervening coherently. Her mother, in spite of her own chequered sexual past, over protects her, and it is a sign of sexual frustration in scene 3 that she dons Yvette's hat and boots and imitates her sexy walk. She is 25 here. Courage is right to insist that there is no safe outlet for her sexuality in army camps, but there is an element of dishonesty in the way she fobs Kattrin off with the promise of marriage after the war, just as their is an element of insensitivity in her attempt to buy her off with the red boots after she has been attacked; it is significant that it is only at this point that Courage reveals that Kattrin's dumbness is the result of being molested by a soldier when she was a baby. Kattrin is still a playful girl in scene 3, 'an entrancing young person' as the Chaplain has it, but she is reduced by scene 7 to a cowering animal, and refuses to show herself when the cook calls her in scene 8. Kattrin's virtue is unselfishness, and it is closely linked with her frustrated maternal instincts, which are all-embracing and naive, where her mother's are perverted by a society that forces her to struggle to survive on its terms. Her love of babies is demonstrated in the shot-up village in scene 5, and it is finally the mention of innocent children that moves Kattrin to climb on the roof and drum out a warning to the sleeping town of Halle in scene 11. She falters, moans when the peasant attacks her mother's waggon, cries when the soldier strikes down the peasant, but, since her response to the situation is rational and intelligent, rather than just emotional, she persists until they kill her. Kattrin's is the only voice consistently raised in defiance of war and war-mongering, and the fact that that 'voice' is dumb provides a strongly ironic symbol.

Kattrin's death is a moment of high pathos, and it demonstrates a positive alternative to Courage's strategy, namely that of individual protest. Within the plot, however, it is an incident, not a liberating solution. Coming as it does towards the end of the play, however, its effect on the audience's final mood is that much stronger. Kattrin's death is not futile in that she succeeds in alerting the sleeping town. But in so far as she is the most perceptive character in the play, her death — and Mother Courage's refusal to be more than momentarily diverted from her business — must be seen as a challenge to the audience to find ways of avoiding the need for such sacrifices in the future.

Supporting characters

The *Chaplain* is a phlegmatic, shifty figure, representing the subordinate role of religion in the Thirty Years War. He is treated with scant respect by the General in scene 2, yet he still plugs the official line that it is a 'war of faith' in scene 3, in spite of the scepticism of Courage and the cook. He assures Courage at some length in scene 6 that the war will survive Tilly's death, because he thinks that is what his breadwinner, as Courage is at this point, wants to hear. Courage brushes aside his proposal of marriage on the pretext that she has no time for personal affairs, but more probably because of his lack of sex-appeal. His conversion to the cause of peace in scene 8 when he calls Courage a hyena of the battlefield is sudden, but it is motivated by his resentment at being displaced by the cook. This is why he vents his spleen on Courage. He is, in the final estimate, a passive, insubstantial figure, toeing the line rather than taking one of his own.

The *cook* is more sharply profiled. He is a suave professional, a hardened campaigner like the recruiters, and like Courage herself. In debunking Gustavus Adolphus's pretext for overruning Poland, he demonstrates an ironic view of life and a sarcastic turn of phrase akin to Brecht's own, and his attitude to women too is not unlike Brecht's own. The cook is offstage between scenes 3 and 8 when Courage is in the Imperial Camp, but we are reminded of him by the Chaplain's jealousy when Courage smokes his pipe in scene 6. A sub-plot that Brecht has prepared almost unnoticed comes to the fore when Yvette unmasks the cook as the man who seduced her years ago — Puffing Piet, who makes love with his pipe clenched between his teeth. But Courage sees him as a kindred spirit and is attracted rather than deterred by his reputation as a womanizer. Their final parting is unsentimental and pragmatic; his inn cannot support three, and she will not be parted from Kattrin and the waggon.

Yvette Pottier is two years younger than Kattrin and serves as a warning to her of the dangers of camp life in scene 3. She lolls around drinking while Kattrin has to work. There is no moral condemnation of the prostitute; she is just trying to make a living in her own special line of business like everybody else. She shows her heart is in the right place when she acts as go-between over Swiss Cheese's ransom. Like the cook she is unseen during Courage's three years with the Imperial troops, but when she reappears in scene 8 she has achieved wealth and rank as Countess Starhemberg. That prostitution should be the only means of self-advancement in the play is a trenchant comment on 17th-century society. She still talks like a soldier's whore, and she is fat and prematurely aged at twenty-five, graphic evidence of the physical price she paid to get where she is.

Epic theatre

The literary term 'epic' is traditionally applied to forms of writing in which the author recounts a story, using as many episodes and characters as a comprehensive account of his subject demands. In modern times the epic has been the preserve of prose fiction, and its standard form the novel. The term 'dramatic' is traditionally applied to forms of writing intended for performance, and these are limited in number of characters and settings by the conventions and resources of the theatre, and in length by the audience's patience and concentration, so that dramatists are in practice restricted to presenting a concentrated plot which shows a conflict and its resolution. The term 'epic theatre', which was first used in Germany in the 1920's and has become firmly associated with the name of Brecht, cuts across the traditional divisions. Epic story-telling is objective; the author stands back from his story as he tells it, and he may interpolate his own comment on events. It was the objectivity and the simultaneous scope for comment in epic writing that attracted the dramatist Brecht, and the beginnings of epic theatre coincide with German experiments in the use of the theatre as an instrument of political instruction.

From the beginning of his career Brecht had fought a running battle against the conventional theatre of his day which he dismissed as 'culinary', since, like expert cooking, it delighted the senses without impinging on the mind. Banners in the auditorium for the production of one of his first plays, *Drums in the Night* in 1922, told the audience not to 'gawp so romantically', and in his essay *On Experimental Theatre* (1939) Brecht asked,

> How can the theatre be entertaining and at the same time instructive? How can it be taken out of the traffic in intellectual drugs and transformed from a place of illusion to a place of insight?

For Brecht the traditional, or dramatic theatre was a place where the audience were absorbed into a comforting illusion which played on their emotions and left them drained, but with a sense of satisfaction which predisposed them to accept the world as they found it. What he himself was looking for was a theatre that would help to change the world.

He first tabulated his ideas on epic theatre in his *Notes on the Opera 'The Rise and Fall of the City of Mahagonny'* (1930) where he set out the contrasts between the dramatic theatre and the epic theatre in a list.

DRAMATIC THEATRE	EPIC THEATRE
plot	narrative
implicates the spectator in a stage situation	turns the spectator into an observer, but
wears down his capacity for action	arouses his capacity for action
provides him with sensations	forces him to take decisions
experience	picture of the world
the spectator is involved in something	he is made to face something
suggestion	argument
instinctive feelings are preserved	brought to the point of recognition
the spectator is in the thick of it, shares the experience	the spectator stands outside, studies
the human being is taken for granted	the human being is the object the inquiry
he is unalterable	he is alterable and able to alter
eyes on the finish	eyes on the course
one scene makes another	each scene for itself
growth	montage
linear development	in curves
evolutionary determinism	jumps
man as a fixed point	man as a process
thought determines being	social being determines thought
feeling	reason

(from *Brecht on Theatre*, p. 37)

The first change of emphasis Brecht advocated was in the manner in which events were presented to the audience. Dramatic theatre enacted plots, involved the audience and stimulated their emotions only to dissipate this active response. Epic theatre was to tell a story in a way that invited the audience to consider the events involved and then to make their own assessment of them. To achieve this, adjustments had to be made to the form of the play. The dramatic play was a closed system of interdependent scenes, each one evolving inexorably from its predecessor, but with the plot so structured that the audience was kept in suspense, wondering how it would all end. The epic play was to be assembled as a montage of independent incidents which showed a process taking place; it would move from scene to scene by curves and jumps, which would keep the audience alert to the way in which things were happening, so that they would finally be able, would indeed be compelled, to judge whether that was the right way. Brecht sometimes compared his plays to scientific experiments; specimens of human behaviour were subjected to scrutiny to see what principles governed them and whether these principles could be improved. Change for the better lay at the centre of Brecht's thinking, and this meant altering the classical notion that the hero of a play should be a fixed character. The conflict between such immutable 'Characters' and their world was the stuff of traditional drama, but Brecht rejected the notion that human nature was fixed, and that man's own thinking governed his being, in favour of a concept of human nature as capable of change. In epic theatre man's thinking is conditioned by his social situation and will change if that changes. At the same time he is the agent of social change, so that there is a constant dialectic, or process of reciprocal influence and change.

The difficulty, at first glance, in relating this to Mother Courage is that she as a character does not change. But in this case this is precisely the point. If the play has been properly presented the audience should have a sinking feeling as she goes off at the end to catch up with business. Everything that has happened to her in the preceding scenes has shown that there is no life for her in that direction, that all her work and good intentions, like the virtues of her children, will be devoured by the framework she knows, accepts and works within, that of a war of exploitation. That framework, like all forms of exploitation, must be changed, and it suffices if the audience realises this, because the play as a political piece has then made its mark.

Mother Courage is a good example of an epic play. It does not develop a conflict in terms of characters, but follows Mother Courage through twelve years, crossing Europe from Scandinavia to Italy and back again to Central Germany to show the effect that her tenacious involvement in the Thirty Years War has on her and her dependants. Between the first and second scenes it jumps from Sweden to Poland for Courage to meet up by chance with her son Eilif again. At the end of scene 3 Courage suppresses every natural feeling to deny her son Swiss Cheese, but at the beginning of scene 4 she is prepared to give vent to her anger at her treatment by the soldiery. She changes her mind when the 'Song of the Grand Capitulation' reminds her that offending the authorities is never good for business. She curses war at the end of scene 6 but right at the beginning of the next scene she is jubilant in its praise. These shifts and changes show Courage in the process of adopting whatever stance her business interests require in the situations as they arise, and they reveal to the audience the false principles that underlie her actions. Courage's story begins long before the play opens and it does not end with the final curtain. She walks off to find more of the same. This kind of open ending is a feature of epic drama.

Brecht would have found this mobile, episodic structure in the 17th-century picaresque novels of Jakob von Grimmelshausen, in one of which, *Trutz Simplex, or the Complete and Wondrous Strange Account of the Life of the Arch-Deceiver and Marauder Courasche* (1670) he found the name of his heroine. Grimmelshausen's most famous novel, *Simplicissimus* (1669), provided Brecht and his production team with their main source of information about everyday life during the Thirty Years War. These novels also had chapter headings telling the reader what was going to happen next. Brecht was familiar with this kind of thing from the inter-shot titles in silent films in the 20's, and he had used scene summaries in a random way before, in *The Threepenny Opera* for example. For *Mother Courage* he worked out a consistent 'titelarium', a set of summaries to be proejcted on a screen or displayed on a banner before each scene. (In the printed play these summaries appear in longer type at the top of each scene.) As well as indicating content, these summaries dated and located the scenes, and related them to History, that is to the great events which Brecht chooses not to show but which his characters carry, as it were, on their backs.

These titles are one of a number of anti-illusionistic devices which Brecht uses to keep the audience on their (metaphorical) toes. From being passive watchers they become intellectually active participants, and the theory is that by being told in advance *what* happens, they are freed to concentrate on *how* it happens. This is one of Brecht's celebrated alienation effects (or 'V-effects' from the German 'Verfremdungseffekte'). Brecht offers the following definition of these,

> What is alienation? To alienate an incident or a character means to take from that incident or character what makes it obvious, familiar or readily understandable, so as to create wonderment and curiosity.

Things are not to be taken for granted but presented in such a way that the audience can criticize them constructively from a social point of view. While the audience at a Brecht production were reading the summaries projected on to screens between the scenes they would be aware of the tops of the properties moving behind the eight feet (2½m.) high Brechtian half-curtain, which ran across the stage on a wire, as the stage crew set up the next scene. Above that they would see the lights hanging from a grid above the stage, and all this would remind them that they were being exposed to the techniques of theatrical presentation, so that they would apply their critical faculties to the events they were seeing. These new techniques were effective in their day because the theatre of illusion had always carefully concealed machinery behind the curtain and cultivated the belief that what the audience saw was somehow a perfect imitation of real life. Brecht's bare grey stage merely had enough scenery and properties to show where the scene was taking place, and to ensure that there was a chair to sit on or a roof to climb on when the text required it; everything was constructed of materials that would have been available on the battlefields of the 17th century. Its sheer starkness came as a surprise to an audience that expected a detailed, realistic set. The bright, white light Brecht used for every scene, regardless of whether it was a spring afternoon in Sweden, or a wintry dawn in the Fichtelgebirge was surprising and sobering too.

Many of these effects have now become conventional — actors walk on and off all the time carrying bits of scenery in the productions of the Royal Shakespeare Company, which never uses a curtain. This means that productions of Brecht's plays which stick slavishly to the models established by the author himself, as those of his own Berliner Ensemble in East Berlin did for many years, can become progressively duller if fresh new equivalents are not found for the original alienation effects.

The use of songs in Brecht's plays constitutes another alienation effect in that the songs are unnatural in the contexts in which they occur. Those in *Mother Courage* are neatly integrated into the action, as has been indicated in the notes. Yvette's 'Song of Fraternisation' and Courage's 'Song of the Grand Capitulation' tell us about the singer's past while at the same time providing wry comment on the way life treated people in the 17th century. The 'Song of Solomon' is a succinct summary of the message of the play, namely that virtue is never rewarded in corrupt times, while at the same time it draws parallels between the fates of famous personages and of Courage and her children. Courage's own song is a trenchant expression of the wolfish principles by which she lives, and Paul Dessau's original music further underscores the falsity of the message.

The songs invite the actors to step out of their roles and address themselves to the audience. The cook does this with a rhetorical flourish when he prefaces the 'Song of Solomon' with 'Ladies and gentlemen, domestic staff and other residents! We are now going to give you . . .' (pp. 74-5). When the actors make this shift, they conform to the general principle of epic acting, that the actor should not identify wholly with his role, any more than he should induce the audience to empathise with it. Brecht explains this in detail in *The Street-Scene: Basic Model for an Epic Theatre*. As a model for the epic actor he uses the example of an eye-witness at a street accident explaining to other passers-by what happened, how the driver and the victim behaved. The eye-witness would demonstrate the sequence of events. He should not get carried away with his role or carry the audience with him into the illusion that they are watching the real event. He does not try to become any of the people involved as he demonstrates their actions, and his own opinion about who was responsible will colour the aspects of the accident he selects and the way he presents them. In the same way the Brechtian 'demonstrative actor' does not try to delude the audience into believing him to have become the person he's playing. And he too will be aware of the social function of his character within the play and will demonstrate his attitude to him in the way he builds up his characterization. If Brecht thought his actors were too involved in their parts he would sometimes require them to say, 'he said' or 'she said' before speaking their lines, to achieve the necessary detachment. It is difficult to imagine how this works with only the printed text to go on, but a concrete example may help. As has been indicated in the notes, Brecht considered that Courage's depravity reaches its lowest point in scene 4 when she dissuades the Young Soldier from making his protest. Nevertheless, when Helene Weigel, in playing this scene showed a glimmer of nobility, Brecht approved, because, as he explains, the depravity is not so much that of her person as that of her class. Helene Weigel managed, it would seem, to demonstrate that while Courage as a social being was behaving as an example of the petite bourgeoisie at its most noxious, as an individual she retained a certain dignity, a hint that in other social circumstances her behaviour would have been different. The point to remember is that empathy is not wanted. Neither the actor nor the audience should identify with the character.

The aim of all Brecht's alienation effects was to reveal character and incident in an unfamiliar light, which would sharpen the audiences attention and stimulate their critical faculties. The dangers of emotion, emotional involvement and seductive illusions are that they blind the audience to the social mechanisms Brecht set in motion before them.

Language

The language of the German original is modern, earthy, popular speech, strongly coloured in Mother Courage's case by the Bavarian dialect one would expect from someone born in Bamberg. The present translation uses a form of northern English as a working equivalent, which is a valid attempt to equate one provincial, no-nonsense idiom with another. The exchanges are hard-hitting and even vulgar, as befits life in an army camp, but they are never obscene. For instance, Mother Courage refers to Yvette's VD obliquely as 'her complaint' (p.22).

Pithy sayings, folk adages, proverbs and biblical allusions abound in the text, though they are frequently used ironically, and some have their validity put to the test. The General invites the Chaplain to comment on 'necessity is the mother of invention' in scene 2, and he has to concede lamely that, though not explicitly Christian, it might just serve as a guideline in wartime. The 'Song of the Grand Capitulation' (pp. 46-7) takes a range of proverbs and lets them cancel one another out. So much for folk wisdom. Its refrain contains one of Brecht's best-known alienations of a well-known phrase. He adjusts the punctuation of 'man proposes, God disposes' to make it read 'man thinks God disposes', and of this there is 'not the faintest chance'. In English this neat shift does not work, and the translator has had to make do with 'Then men swear God's there', which is weak by comparison, but then translating Brecht's deft linguistic tricks is near impossible.

Staging

In Brecht's Berlin production the play opened with the recruiters standing on a bare grey stage, on to which Courage's wagon was hauled. The waggon then remained the most prominent element on the stage throughout the play, and its equipment and state of repair varied with the prosperity of her business. The stage was framed with huge screens made of tenting stretched between wooden poles which were lashed together with ropes, all materials that would have been available on a 17th-century military encampment. Brecht always insisted on the texture of reality, which meant that the materials used for the costumes and set not only had to be authentic, they also had to show signs of the wear and tear of daily use. Where buildings such as the parsonage and the peasant's house were required, only the part that the action required was built, but here too the materials were authentic. The peasant's house in scene 11, for example, consisted only of a front door and a porch with a sloping roof, supported by two rough square pillars, so that Kattrin could climb on this with her drum. Again, this approach to scenery has become commonplace in the theatre today but was innovative in Brecht's time.

At the end Courage's battered waggon stood on the same bare stage as at the beginning, only now the bareness symbolized the measureless devastation into which the war had led her, and not the wide horizons open to her. She trudges off, the stage revolving slowly against her. Brecht set the revolve in motion repeatedly throughout the play to enable Courage and her entourage to trudge forward without making much real headway.

Further reading

Bertolt Brecht: *Brecht on Theatre* (translation and notes by John Willett), Eyre Methuen, London, 1964. Brecht's essential theoretical and critical writings assembled in one handy volume.

Graham Bartram and Anthony Waine: *Brecht in Perspective*, Longman, London and New York, 1982. Essays by British scholars which examine Brecht's literary, historical and social background, relate him to the German theatrical tradition, and compare him with seminal figures like Piscator and Stanislavsky.

Keith A. Dickson: *Towards Utopia*, Oxford University Press, 1978. Closely argued study of Brecht and his work which draws on research in English, German and Russian. Dickson pursues the utopian vision behind Brecht's satirical presentation of life. The book is organized around themes (Man and Society, the Historical Perspective, etc.) and deals with plays, poetry and prose.

Martin Esslin: *Brecht: a Choice of Evils,* 3rd ed., Eyre Methuen, London, 1980. An early appraisal with useful insights, in spite of the writer's obvious antipathy to Brecht's politics.

Ronald Gray: *Brecht the Dramatist*, Cambridge University Press, 1976. A chronological and somewhat severe examination of the plays. He singles out the intensity with which Brecht probes moral and social problems as the dramatist's best feature. There is a thought-provoking chapter on *Courage*.

Claude Hill: *Bertolt Brecht*, Twayne, Boston, 1975. An American survey, clear and useful, with separate chapters on major works.

Jan Needle and Peter Thompson: *Brecht*, Blackwell, Oxford, 1981. The authors have studied Brecht in English translation. They are best on the plays in performance, offering an illuminating account of Brecht's 'Model-Book' for *Courage*.

Alfred D. White: *Bertolt Brecht's Great Plays*, Macmillan, London, 1978. Analyses of the major plays in separate chapters.

John Willett: *The Theatre of Bertolt Brecht*, 4th ed., Eyre Methuen, London, 1977. Seminal compendium of basic information.

All Brecht's major plays (and many minor works) are published in English translation in the Methuen Modern Plays series. Also published by Methuen are volumes of Brecht's *Poems 1913-56, Short Stories 1921-46* and *Diaries 1920-22.*

Mother Courage and Her Children

Translator: JOHN WILLETT

Characters

MOTHER COURAGE
KATTRIN, *her dumb daughter*
EILIF, *the elder son*
SWISS CHEESE, *the younger son*
THE RECRUITER
THE SERGEANT
THE COOK
THE GENERAL
THE CHAPLAIN
THE ARMOURER
YVETTE POTTIER
THE MAN WITH THE PATCH
ANOTHER SERGEANT
THE ANCIENT COLONEL
A CLERK
A YOUNG SOLDIER
AN OLDER SOLDIER
A PEASANT
THE PEASANT'S WIFE
THE YOUNG MAN
THE OLD WOMAN
ANOTHER PEASANT
HIS WIFE
THE YOUNG PEASANT
THE ENSIGN
Soldiers
A Voice

I

Spring 1624. The Swedish Commander-in-Chief
Count Oxenstierna is raising troops in Dalecarlia
for the Polish campaign. The canteen woman
Anna Fierling, known under the name of Mother
Courage, loses one son

Country road near a town.
A sergeant and a recruiter stand shivering.

RECRUITER: How can you muster a unit in a place like this?
I've been thinking about suicide, Sergeant. Here am I, got
to find our commander four companies before the twelfth
of the month, and people round here are so nasty I can't
sleep nights. S'pose I get hold of some bloke and shut my
eye to his pigeon chest and varicose veins, I get him proper
drunk, he signs on the line, I'm just settling up, he goes for
a piss, I follow him to the door because I smell a rat; bob's
your uncle, he's off like a flea with the itch. No notion of
word of honour, loyalty, faith, sense of duty. This place
has shattered my confidence in the human race, sergeant.

SERGEANT: It's too long since they had a war here; stands to
reason. Where's their sense of morality to come from?
Peace – that's just a mess; takes a war to restore order.
Peacetime, the human race runs wild. People and cattle get
buggered about, who cares? Everyone eats just as he feels
inclined, a hunk of cheese on top of his nice white bread,
and a slice of fat on top of the cheese. How many young
blokes and good horses in that town there, nobody knows;
they never thought of counting. I been in places ain't seen

a war for nigh seventy years: folks hadn't got names to them, couldn't tell one another apart. Takes a war to get proper nominal rolls and inventories – shoes in bundles and corn in bags, and man and beast properly numbered and carted off, cause it stands to reason: no order, no war.

RECRUITER: Too true.

SERGEANT: Same with all good things, it's a job to get a war going. But once it's blossomed out there's no holding it; folk start fighting shy of peace like punters what can't stop for fear of having to tot up what they lost. Before that it's war they're fighting shy of. It's something new to them.

RECRUITER: Hey, here's a cart coming. Two tarts with two young fellows. Stop her, sergeant. If this one's a flop I'm not standing around in your spring winds any longer, I can tell you.

Sound of a jew's-harp. Drawn by two young fellows, a covered cart rolls in. On it sit Mother Courage and her dumb daughter Kattrin.

MOTHER COURAGE: Morning, sergeant.

SERGEANT *blocking the way*: Morning, all And who are you?

MOTHER COURAGE: Business folk. *Sings*:

You captains, tell the drums to slacken
And give your infanteers a break:
It's Mother Courage with her waggon
Full of the finest boots they make.
With crawling lice and looted cattle
With lumbering guns and straggling kit –
How can you flog them into battle
Unless you get them boots that fit?

The new year's come. The watchmen shout.
The thaw sets in. The dead remain.
Wherever life has not died out
It staggers to its feet again.

Captains, how can you make them face it –
Marching to death without a brew?

Courage has rum with which to lace it
And boil their souls and bodies through.
Their musket primed, their stomach hollow –
Captains, your men don't look so well.
So feed them up and let them follow
While you command them into hell.
     The new year's come. The watchmen shout.
     The thaw sets in. The dead remain.
     Wherever life has not died out
     It staggers to its feet again.

SERGEANT: Halt! Who are you with, you trash?

THE ELDER SON: Second Finnish Regiment.

SERGEANT: Where's your papers?

MOTHER COURAGE: Papers?

THE YOUNGER SON: What, mean to say you don't know Mother Courage?

SERGEANT: Never heard of her. What's she called Courage for?

MOTHER COURAGE: Courage is the name they gave me because I was scared of going broke, sergeant, so I drove me cart right through the bombardment of Riga with fifty loaves of bread aboard. They were going mouldy, it was high time, hadn't any choice really.

SERGEANT: Don't be funny with me. Your papers.

MOTHER COURAGE *pulling a bundle of papers from a tin box and climbing down off the cart*: That's all my papers, sergeant. You'll find a whole big missal from Altötting in Bavaria for wrapping gherkins in, and a road map of Moravia, the Lord knows when I'll ever get there, might as well chuck it away, and here's a stamped certificate that my horse hasn't got foot-and-mouth, only he's dead worse luck, cost fifteen florins he did – not me luckily. That enough paper for you?

SERGEANT: You pulling my leg? I'll knock that sauce out of you. S'pose you know you got to have a licence.

MOTHER COURAGE: Talk proper to me, do you mind, and don't you dare say I'm pulling your leg in front of my unsullied children, 'tain't decent, I got no time for you. My honest face, that's me licence with the Second Regiment, and if it's too difficult for you to read there's nowt I can do about it. Nobody's putting a stamp on that.

RECRUITER: Sergeant, methinks I smell insubordination in this individual. What's needed in our camp is obedience.

MOTHER COURAGE: Sausage, if you ask me.

SERGEANT: Name.

MOTHER COURAGE: Anna Fierling.

SERGEANT: You all called Fierling then?

MOTHER COURAGE: What d'you mean? It's me's called Fierling, not them.

SERGEANT: Aren't all this lot your children?

MOTHER COURAGE: You bet they are, but why should they all have to be called the same, eh? *Pointing to her elder son:* For instance, that one's called Eilif Nojocki – Why? his father always claimed he was called Kojocki or Mojocki or something. The boy remembers him clearly, except that the one he remembers was someone else, a Frenchie with a little beard. Aside from that he's got his father's wits; that man knew how to snitch a peasant's pants off his bum without him noticing. This way each of us has his own name, see.

SERGEANT: What, each one different?

MOTHER COURAGE: Don't tell me you ain't never come across that.

SERGEANT: So I s'pose he's a Chinaman? *Pointing to the younger son.*

MOTHER COURAGE: Wrong. Swiss.

SERGEANT: After the Frenchman?

MOTHER COURAGE: What Frenchman? I never heard tell of no Frenehman. You keep muddling things up, we'll be hanging around here till dark. A Swiss, but called Fejos, and the name has nowt to do with his father. He was called something quite different and was a fortifications engineer, only drunk all the time.

Swiss Cheese beams and nods; dumb Kattrin too is amused.

SERGEANT: How in hell can he be called Fejos?

MOTHER COURAGE: I don't like to be rude, sergeant, but you ain't got much imagination, have you? Course he's called Fejos, because when he arrived I was with a Hungarian, very decent fellow, had terrible kidney trouble though he never touched a drop. The boy takes after him.

SERGEANT: But he wasn't his father . . .

MOTHER COURAGE: Took after him just the same. I call him Swiss Cheese. *Pointing to her daughter:* And that's Kattrin Haupt, she's half German.

SERGEANT: Nice family, I must say.

MOTHER COURAGE: Aye, me cart and me have seen the world.

SERGEANT: I'm writing all this down. *He writes.* And you're from Bamberg in Bavaria; how d'you come to be here?

MOTHER COURAGE: Can't wait till war chooses to visit Bamberg, can I?

RECRUITER *to Eilif:* You two should be called Jacob Ox and Esau Ox, pulling the cart like that. I s'pose you never get out of harness?

EILIF: Ma, can I clobber him one? I wouldn't half like to.

MOTHER COURAGE: And I says you can't; just you stop where you are. And now two fine officers like you, I bet you could use a good pistol, or a belt buckle, yours is on its last legs, sergeant.

SERGEANT: I could use something else. Those boys are healthy as young birch trees, I observe: chests like barrels, solid leg muscles. So why are they dodging their military service, may I ask?

MOTHER COURAGE *quickly:* Nowt doing, sergeant. Yours is no trade for my kids.

RECRUITER: But why not? There's good money in it, glory

too. Flogging boots is women's work. *To Eilif:* Come here, let's see if you've muscles in you or if you're a chicken.

MOTHER COURAGE: He's a chicken. Give him a fierce look, he'll fall over.

RECRUITER: Killing a young bull that happens to be in his way. *Wants to lead him off*.

MOTHER COURAGE: Let him alone, will you? He's nowt for you folk.

RECRUITER: He was crudely offensive and talked about clobbering me. The two of us are going to step into that field and settle it man to man.

EILIF: Don't you worry, mum, I'll fix him.

MOTHER COURAGE: Stop there! You varmint! I know you, nowt but fights. There's a knife down his boot. A slasher, that's what he is.

RECRUITER: I'll draw it out of him like a milk-tooth. Come along, sonny.

MOTHER COURAGE: Sergeant, I'll tell the colonel. He'll have you both in irons. The lieutenant's going out with my daughter.

SERGEANT: No rough stuff, chum. *To Mother Courage:* What you got against military service? Wasn't his own father a soldier? Died a soldier's death, too? Said it yourself.

MOTHER COURAGE: He's nowt but a child. You want to take him off to slaughterhouse, I know you lot. They'll give you five florins for him.

RECRUITER: First he's going to get a smart cap and boots, eh?

EILIF: Not from you.

MOTHER COURAGE: Let's both go fishing, said angler to worm. *To Swiss Cheese:* Run off, call out they're trying to kidnap your brother. *She pulls a knife:* Go on, you kidnap him, just try. I'll slit you open, trash. I'll teach you to make war with him. We're doing an honest trade in ham and linen, and we're peaceable folk.

SERGEANT: Peaceable I don't think; look at your knife. You should be ashamed of yourself; put that knife away, you old harridan. A minute back you were admitting you live off the war, how else should you live, what from? But how's anyone to have war without soldiers?

MOTHER COURAGE: No need for it to be my kids.

SERGEANT: Oh, you'd like war to eat the pips but spit out the apple? It's to fatten up your kids, but you won't invest in it. Got to look after itself, eh? And you called Courage, fancy that. Scared of the war that keeps you going? Your sons aren't scared of it, I can see that.

EILIF: Take more than a war to scare me.

SERGEANT: And why? Look at me: has army life done all that badly by me? Joined up at seventeen.

MOTHER COURAGE: Still got to reach seventy.

SERGEANT: I don't mind waiting.

MOTHER COURAGE: Under the sod, eh?

SERGEANT: You trying to insult me, saying I'll die?

MOTHER COURAGE: S'pose it's true? S'pose I can see the mark's on you? S'pose you look like a corpse on leave to me? Eh?

SWISS CHEESE: She's got second sight, Mother has.

RECRUITER: Go ahead, tell the sergeant's fortune, might amuse him.

MOTHER COURAGE: Gimme helmet. *He gives it to her.*

SERGEANT: It don't mean a bloody sausage. Anything for a laugh though.

MOTHER COURAGE *taking out a sheet of parchment and tearing it up*: Eilif, Swiss Cheese and Kattrin, may all of us be torn apart like this if we lets ourselves get too mixed up in the war. *To the Sergeant:* Just for you I'm doing it for free. Black's for death. I'm putting a big black cross on this slip of paper.

SWISS CHEESE: Leaving the other one blank, see?

MOTHER COURAGE: Then I fold them across and shake

them. All of us is jumbled together like this from our mother's womb, and now draw a slip and you'll know. *The Sergeant hesitates.*

RECRUITER *to Eilif*: I don't take just anybody, they all know I'm choosey, but you got the kind of fire I like to see.

SERGEANT *fishing in the helmet*: Too silly. Load of eyewash.

SWISS CHEESE: Drawn a black cross, he has. Write him off.

RECRUITER: They're having you on; not everybody's name's on a bullet.

SERGEANT *hoarsely*: You've put me in the shit.

MOTHER COURAGE: Did that yourself the day you became a soldier. Come along, let's move on now. 'Tain't every day we have a war, I got to get stirring.

SERGEANT: God damn it, you can't kid me. We're taking that bastard of yours for a soldier.

EILIF: Swiss Cheese'd like to be a soldier too.

MOTHER COURAGE: First I've heard of that. You'll have to draw too, all three of you. *She goes to the rear to mark crosses on further slips.*

RECRUITER *to Eilif*: One of the things they say against us is that it's all holy-holy in the Swedish camp; but that's a malicious rumour to do us down. There's no hymn-singing but Sundays, just a single verse, and then only for those got voices.

MOTHER COURAGE *coming back with the slips, which she drops into the sergeant's helmet*: Trying to get away from their ma, the devils, off to war like calves to salt-lick. But I'm making you draw lots, and that'll show you the world is no vale of joys with 'Come along, son, we need a few more generals'. Sergeant, I'm so scared they won't get through the war. Such dreadful characters, all three of them. *She hands the helmet to Eilif.* Hey, come on, fish out your slip. *He fishes one out, unfolds it. She snatches it from him.* There you are, it's a cross. Oh, wretched mother that I am, o pain-racked giver of birth! Shall he die? Aye, in the springtime of life he is doomed. If he becomes a soldier he shall bite the dust, it's plain to see. He is too foolhardy, like his dad was. And if he ain't sensible he'll go the way of all flesh, his slip proves it. *Shouts at him*: You going to be sensible?

EILIF: Why not?

MOTHER COURAGE: Sensible thing is stay with your mother, never mind if they poke fun at you and call you chicken, just you laugh.

RECRUITER: If you're pissing in your pants I'll make do with your brother.

MOTHER COURAGE: I told you laugh. Go on, laugh. Now you draw, Swiss Cheese. I'm not so scared on your account, you're honest. *He fishes in the helmet*. Oh, why look at your slip in that strange way? It's got to be a blank. There can't be any cross on it. Surely I'm not going to lose *you*. *She takes the slip*. A cross? What, you too? Is that because you're so simple, perhaps? O Swiss Cheese, you too will be sunk if you don't stay utterly honest all the while, like I taught you from childhood when you brought the change back from the baker's. Else you can't save yourself. Look, sergeant, that's a black cross, ain't it?

SERGEANT: A cross, that's right. Can't think how I come to get one. I always stay in the rear. *To the Recruiter:* There's no catch. Her own family get it too.

SWISS CHEESE: I get it too. But I listen to what I'm told.

MOTHER COURAGE *to Kattrin*: And now you're the only one I know's all right, you're a cross yourself; got a kind heart you have. *Holds the helmet up to her on the cart, but takes the slip out herself*. No, that's too much. That can't be right; must have made a mistake shuffling. Don't be too kind-hearted, Kattrin, you'll have to give it up, there's a cross above your path too. Lie doggo, girl, it can't be that hard once you're born dumb, Right, all of you know now. Look out for yourselves, you'll need to. And now up we get and on we go. *She climbs on to the cart.*

RECRUITER *to the sergeant*: Do something.

SERGEANT: I don't feel very well.

RECRUITER: Must of caught a chill taking your helmet off in that wind. Involve her in a deal. *Aloud:* Might as well have a look at that belt-buckle, sergeant. After all, our friends here have to live by their business. Hey, you people, the sergeant wants to buy that belt-buckle.

MOTHER COURAGE: Half a florin. Two florins is what a belt like that's worth. *Climbs down again.*

SERGEANT: 'Tain't new. Let me get out of this damned wind and have a proper look at it. *Goes behind the cart with the buckle.*

MOTHER COURAGE: Ain't what I call windy.

SERGEANT: I s'pose it might be worth half a florin, it's silver.

MOTHER COURAGE *joining him behind the cart*: It's six solid ounces.

RECRUITER *to Eilif*: And then we men'll have one together. Got your bounty money here, come along. *Eilif stands undecided.*

MOTHER COURAGE: Half a florin it is.

SERGEANT: It beats me. I'm always at the rear. Sergeant's the safest job there is. You can send the others up front, cover themselves with glory. Me dinner hour's properly spoiled. Shan't be able to hold nowt down, I know.

MOTHER COURAGE: Mustn't let it prey on you so's you can't eat. Just stay at the rear. Here, take a swig of brandy, man. *Gives him a drink.*

RECRUITER *has taken Eilif by the arm and is leading him away up stage*: Ten florins bounty money, then you're a gallant fellow fighting for the king and women'll be after you like flies. And you can clobber me for free for insulting you. *Exeunt both.*

Dumb Kattrin leans down from the cart and makes hoarse noises.

MOTHER COURAGE: All right, Kattrin, all right. Sergeant's just paying. *Bites the half-florin.* I got no faith in any kind of money. Burnt child, that's me, sergeant. This coin's good, though. And now let's get moving. Where's Eilif?

SWISS CHEESE: Went off with the recruiter.

MOTHER COURAGE *stands quite still, then*: You simpleton. *To Kattrin*: 'Tain't your fault, you can't speak, I know.

SERGEANT: Could do with a swig yourself, ma. That's life. Plenty worse things than being a soldier. Want to live off war, but keep yourself and family out of it, eh?

MOTHER COURAGE: You'll have to help your brother pull now, Kattrin.

Brother and sister hitch themselves to the cart and start pulling. Mother Courage walks alongside. The cart rolls on.

SERGEANT *looking after them*:

Like the war to nourish you?
Have to feed it something too.

2

In the years 1625 and 1626 Mother Courage crosses Poland in the train of the Swedish armies. Before the fortress of Wallhof she meets her son again. Successful sale of a capon and heyday of her dashing son

The general's tent.

Beside it, his kitchen. Thunder of cannon. The cook is arguing with Mother Courage, who wants to sell him a capon.

THE COOK: Sixty hellers for a miserable bird like that?

MOTHER COURAGE: Miserable bird? This fat brute? Mean

to say some greedy old general – and watch your step if you got nowt for his dinner – can't afford sixty hellers for him?

THE COOK: I can get a dozen like that for ten hellers just down the road.

MOTHER COURAGE: What, a capon like this you can get just down the road? In time of siege, which means hunger that tears your guts. A rat you might get: 'might' I say because they're all being gobbled up, five men spending best part of day chasing one hungry rat. Fifty hellers for a giant capon in time of siege!

THE COOK: But it ain't us having the siege, it's t'other side. We're conducting the siege, can't you get that in your head?

MOTHER COURAGE: But we got nowt to eat too, even worse than them in the town. Took it with them, didn't they? They're having a high old time, everyone says. And look at us! I been to the peasants, there's nowt there.

THE COOK: There's plenty. They're sitting on it.

MOTHER COURAGE *triumphantly*: They ain't. They're bust, that's what they are. Just about starving. I saw some, were grubbing up roots from sheer hunger, licking their fingers after they boiled some old leather strap. That's way it is. And me got a capon here and supposed to take forty hellers for it.

THE COOK: Thirty, not forty. I said thirty.

MOTHER COURAGE: Here, this ain't just any old capon. It was such a gifted beast, I been told, it could only eat to music, had a military march of its own. It could count, it was that intelligent. And you say forty hellers is too much? General will make mincemeat of you if there's nowt on his table.

THE COOK: See what I'm doing? *He takes a piece of beef and puts his knife to it.* Here I got a bit of beef, I'm going to roast it. Make up your mind quick.

MOTHER COURAGE: Go on, roast it. It's last year's.

THE COOK: Last night's. That animal was still alive and kicking, I saw him myself.

MOTHER COURAGE: Alive and stinking, you mean.

THE COOK: I'll cook him five hours if need be. I'll just see if he's still tough. *He cuts into it.*

MOTHER COURAGE: Put plenty of pepper on it so his lordship the general don't smell the pong.

The general, a chaplain and Eilif enter the tent.

THE GENERAL *slapping Eilif on the shoulder*: Now then, Eilif my son, into your general's tent with you and sit thou at my right hand. For you accomplished a deed of heroism, like a pious cavalier; and doing what you did for God, and in a war of religion at that, is something I commend in you most highly, you shall have a gold bracelet as soon as we've taken this town. Here we are, come to save their souls for them, and what do those insolent dung-encrusted yokels go and do? Drive their beef away from us. They stuff it into those priests of theirs all right, back and front, but you taught 'em manners, ha! So here's a pot of red wine for you, the two of us'll knock it back at one gulp. *They do so.* Piss all for the chaplain, the old bigot. And now, what would you like for dinner, my darling?

EILIF: A bit of meat, why not?

THE GENERAL: Cook! Meat!

THE COOK: And then he goes and brings guests when there's nowt there.

Mother Courage silences him so she can listen.

EILIF: Hungry job cutting down peasants.

MOTHER COURAGE: Jesus Christ, it's my Eilif.

THE COOK: Your what?

MOTHER COURAGE: My eldest boy. It's two years since I lost sight of him, they pinched him from me on the road, must think well of him if the general's asking him to dinner, and what kind of a dinner can you offer? Nowt. You heard what the visitor wishes to eat: meat. Take my tip, you settle for the capon, it'll be a florin.

THE GENERAL *has sat down with Eilif, and bellows*: Food, Lamb, you foul cook, or I'll have your hide.

THE COOK: Give it over, dammit, this is blackmail.

MOTHER COURAGE: Didn't someone say it was a miserable bird?

THE COOK: Miserable; give it over, and a criminal price, fifty hellers.

MOTHER COURAGE: A florin, I said. For my eldest boy, the general's guest, no expense is too great for me.

THE COOK *gives her the money*: You might at least pluck it while I see to the fire.

MOTHER COURAGE *sits down to pluck the fowl*: He won't half be surprised to see me. He's my dashing clever son. Then I got a stupid one too, he's honest though. The girl's nowt. One good thing, she don't talk.

THE GENERAL: Drink up, my son, this is my best Falernian; only got a barrel or two left, but that's nothing to pay for a sign that's there's still true faith to be found in my army. As for that shepherd of souls he can just look on, because all he does is preach, without the least idea how it's to be carried out. And now, my son Eilif, tell us more about the neat way you smashed those yokels and captured the twenty oxen. Let's hope they get here soon.

EILIF: A day or two at most.

MOTHER COURAGE: Thoughtful of our Eilif not to bring the oxen in till tomorrow, else you lot wouldn't have looked twice at my capon.

EILIF: Well, it was like this, see. I'd heard peasants had been driving the oxen they'd hidden, out of the forest into one particular wood, on the sly and mostly by night. That's where people from the town were s'posed to come and pick them up. So I holds off and lets them drive their oxen together, reckoning they'd be better than me at finding 'em.

I had my blokes slavering after the meat, cut their emer-
gency rations even further for a couple of days till their
mouths was watering at the least sound of any word
beginning with 'me-', like 'measles' say.

THE GENERAL: Very clever of you.

EILIF: Possibly. The rest was a piece of cake. Except that the
peasants had cudgels and outnumbered us three to one and
made a murderous attack on us. Four of 'em shoved me into
a thicket, knocked my sword from my hand and bawled out
'Surrender!' What's the answer, I wondered; they're going
to make mincemeat of me.

THE GENERAL: What did you do?

EILIF: I laughed.

THE GENERAL: You did what?

EILIF: Laughed. So we got talking. I put it on a business
footing from the start, told them 'Twenty florins a head's
too much. I'll give you fifteen'. As if I was meaning to pay.
That threw them, and they began scratching their heads. In
a flash I'd picked up my sword and was hacking 'em to
pieces. Necessity's the mother of invention, eh, sir?

THE GENERAL: What is your view, pastor of souls?

THE CHAPLAIN: That phrase is not strictly speaking in the
Bible, but when Our Lord turned the five loaves into five
hundred there was no war on and he could tell people to
love their neighbours as they'd had enough to eat. Today
it's another story.

THE GENERAL *laughs*: Quite another story. You can have a
swig after all for that, you old Pharisee. *To Eilif*: Hacked
'em to pieces, did you, so my gallant lads can get a proper
bite to eat? What do the Scriptures say? 'Whatsoever thou
doest for the least of my brethren, thou doest for me'. And
what did you do for them? Got them a good square meal
of beef, because they're not accustomed to mouldy bread,
the old way was to fix a cold meal of rolls and wine in your
helmet before you went out to fight for God.

EILIF: Aye, in a flash I'd picked up my sword and was hacking them to pieces.

THE GENERAL: You've the makings of a young Caesar. You ought to see the King.

EILIF: I have from a distance. He kind of glows. I'd like to model myself on him.

THE GENERAL: You've got something in common already. I appreciate soldiers like you, Eilif, men of courage. Somebody like that I treat as I would my own son. *He leads him over to the map.* Have a look at the situation, Eilif; it's a long haul still.

MOTHER COURAGE *who has been listening and now angrily plucks the fowl*: That must be a rotten general.

THE COOK: He's ravenous all right, but why rotten?

MOTHER COURAGE: Because he's got to have men of courage, that's why. If he knew how to plan a proper campaign what would he be needing men of courage for? Ordinary ones would do. It's always the same; whenever there's a load of special virtues around it means something stinks.

THE COOK: I thought it meant things is all right.

MOTHER COURAGE: No, that they stink. Look, s'pose some general or king is bone stupid and leads his men up shit creek, then those men've got to be fearless, there's another virtue for you. S'pose he's stingy and hires too few soldiers, then they got to be a crowd of Hercules's. And s'pose he's slapdash and don't give a bugger, then they got to be clever as monkeys else their number's up. Same way they got to show exceptional loyalty each time he gives them impossible jobs. Nowt but virtues no proper country and no decent king or general would ever need. In decent countries folk don't have to have virtues, the whole lot can be perfectly ordinary, average intelligence, and for all I know cowards.

THE GENERAL: I'll wager your father was a soldier.

EILIF: A great soldier, I been told. My mother warned me about it. There's a song I know.

THE GENERAL: Sing it to us. *Roars:* When's that dinner coming?

EILIF: It's called The Song of the Girl and the Soldier.
He sings it, dancing a war dance with his sabre:

> The guns blaze away, and the bay'nit'll slay
> And the water can't hardly be colder.
> What's the answer to ice? Keep off's my advice!
> That's what the girl told the soldier.
> Next thing the soldier, wiv' a round up the spout
> Hears the band playing and gives a great shout:
> Why, it's marching what makes you a soldier!
> So it's down to the south and then northwards once more:
> See him catching that bay'nit in his naked paw!
> That's what his comrades done told her.
>
> Oh, do not despise the advice of the wise
> Learn wisdom from those that are older
> And don't try for things that are out of your reach –
> That's what the girl told the soldier.
> Next thing the soldier, his bay'nit in place
> Wades into the river and laughs in her face
> Though the water comes up to his shoulder.
> When the shingle roof glints in the light o' the moon
> We'll be wiv' you again, not a moment too soon!
> That's what his comrades done told her.

MOTHER COURAGE *takes up the song in the kitchen, beating on a pot with her spoon:*

> You'll go out like a light! And the sun'll take flight
> For your courage just makes us feel colder.
> Oh, that vanishing light! May God see that it's right! –
> That's what the girl told the soldier.

EILIF: What's that?

MOTHER COURAGE *continues singing*:

> Next thing the soldier, his bay'nit in place
> Was caught by the current and went down without trace
> And the water couldn't hardly be colder.
> The the shingle roof froze in the light o' the moon
> As both soldier and ice drifted down to their doom –
> And d'you know what his comrades done told her?
>
> He went out like a light. And the sunshine took flight
> For his courage just made 'em feel colder.
> Oh, do not despise the advice of the wise!
> That's what the girl told the soldier.

THE GENERAL: The things they get up to in my kitchen these days.

EILIF *has gone into the kitchen. He flings his arms round his mother*: Fancy seeing you again, ma! Where's the others?

MOTHER COURAGE *in his arms*: Snug as a bug in a rug. They made Swiss Cheese paymaster of the Second Finnish; any road he'll stay out of fighting that way, I couldn't keep him out altogether.

EILIF: How's the old feet?

MOTHER COURAGE: Bit tricky getting me shoes on of a morning.

THE GENERAL *has joined them*: So you're his mother, I hope you've got plenty more sons for me like this one.

EILIF: Ain't it my lucky day? You sitting out there in the kitchen, ma, hearing your son commended . . .

MOTHER COURAGE: You bet I heard. *Slaps his face.*

EILIF *holding his cheek*: What's that for? Taking the oxen?

MOTHER COURAGE: No. Not surrendering when those four went for you and wanted to make mincemeat of you. Didn't I say you should look after yourself? You Finnish devil!

The general and the chaplain stand in the doorway laughing.

3

Three years later Mother Courage is taken prisoner along with elements of a Finnish regiment. She manages to save her daughter, likewise her covered cart, but her honest son is killed

Military camp.
Afternoon. A flagpole with the regimental flag. From her cart, festooned now with all kinds of goods, Mother Courage has stretched a washing line to a large cannon, across which she and Kattrin are folding the washing. She is bargaining at the same time with an armourer over a sack of shot. Swiss Cheese, now wearing a paymaster's uniform, is looking on.

A comely person, Yvette Pottier, is sewing a gaily coloured hat, a glass of brandy before her. She is in her stockinged feet, having laid aside her red high-heeled boots.

THE ARMOURER: I'll let you have that shot for a couple of florins. It's cheap at the price, I got to have the money because the colonel's been boozing with his officers since two days back, and the drink's run out.

MOTHER COURAGE: That's troops' munitions. They catch me with that, I'm for court-martial. You crooks flog the shot, and troops got nowt to fire at enemy.

THE ARMOURER: Have a heart, can't you; you scratch my back and I'll scratch yours.

MOTHER COURAGE: I'm not taking army property. Not at that price.

THE ARMOURER: You can sell it on the q.t. tonight to the Fourth Regiment's armourer for five florins, eight even, if you let him have a receipt for twelve. He's right out of ammunition.

MOTHER COURAGE: Why not you do it?

THE ARMOURER: I don't trust him, he's a pal of mine.

MOTHER COURAGE *takes the sack*: Gimme. *To Kattrin:* Take it away and pay him a florin and a half. *The armourer protests.* I said a florin and a half. *Kattrin drags the sack upstage, the armourer following her. Mother Courage addresses Swiss Cheese:* Here's your woollies, now look after them, it's October and autumn may set in any time. I ain't saying it's got to, cause I've learned nowt's got to come when you think it will, not even seasons of the year. But your regimental accounts got to add up right, come what may. Do they add up right?

SWISS CHEESE: Yes, mother.

MOTHER COURAGE: Don't you forget they made you pay-master cause you was honest, not dashing like your brother, and above all so stupid I bet you ain't even thought of clearing off with it, no not you. That's a big consolation to me. And don't lose those woollies.

SWISS CHEESE: No, mother, I'll put them under my mattress. *Begins to go.*

THE ARMOURER: I'll go along with you, paymaster.

MOTHER COURAGE: And don't you start learning him none of your tricks.

The armourer leaves with Swiss Cheese without any farewell gesture.

YVETTE *waving to him*: No reason not to say goodbye, armourer.

MOTHER COURAGE *to Yvette*: I don't like to see them together. He's wrong company for our Swiss Cheese. Oh well, war's off to a good start. Easily take four, five years before all countries are in. A bit of foresight, don't do nothing silly, and business'll flourish. Don't you know you ain't s'posed to drink before midday with your complaint?

YVETTE: Complaint, who says so, it's a libel.

MOTHER COURAGE: They all say so.

YVETTE: Because they're all telling lies, Mother Courage, and me at my wits' end cause they're all avoiding me like something the cat brought in thanks to those lies, what the hell am I remodelling my hat for? *She throws it away.* That's why I drink before midday. Never used to, gives you crows' feet, but now what the hell? All the Second Finnish know me. Ought to have stayed at home when my first fellow did me wrong. No good our sort being proud. Eat shit, that's what you got to do, or down you go.

MOTHER COURAGE: Now don't you start up again about that Pieter of yours and how it all happened, in front of my innocent daughter too.

YVETTE: She's the one should hear it, put her off love.

MOTHER COURAGE: Nobody can put 'em off that.

YVETTE: Then I'll go on, get it off my chest. It all starts with yours truly growing up in lovely Flanders, else I'd never of seen him and wouldn't be stuck here now in Poland, cause he was an army cook, fair-haired, a Dutchman but thin for once. Kattrin, watch out for the thin ones, only in those days I didn't know that, or that he'd got a girl already, or that they all called him Puffing Piet cause he never took his pipe out of his mouth when he was on the job, it meant that little to him. *She sings the Song of Fraternisation:*

> When I was only sixteen
> The foe came into our land.
> He laid aside his sabre
> And with a smile he took my hand.
> After the May parade
> The May light starts to fade.
> The regiment dressed by the right
> The drums were beaten, that's the drill.
> The foe took us behind the hill
> And fraternised all night.

There were so many foes then
But mine worked in the mess.
I loathed him in the daytime.
At night I loved him none the less.
After the May parade
The May light starts to fade.
The regiment dressed by the right
The drums were beaten, that's the drill.
The foe took us behind the hill
And fraternised all night.

The love which came upon me
Was wished on me by fate.
My friends could never grasp why
I found it hard to share their hate.
The fields were wet with dew
When sorrow first I knew.
The regiment dressed by the right
The drums were beaten, that's the drill.
And then the foe, my lover still
Went marching out of sight.

I followed him, fool that I was, but I never found him, and that was five years back. *She walks unsteadily behind the cart.*

MOTHER COURAGE: You left your hat here.

YVETTE: Anyone wants it can have it.

MOTHER COURAGE: Let that be a lesson, Kattrin. Don't you start anything with them soldiers. Love makes the world go round, I'm warning you. Even with fellows not in the army it's no bed of roses. He says he'd like to kiss the ground your feet walk on – reminds me, did you wash them yesterday? – and after that you're his skivvy. Be thankful you're dumb, then you can't contradict yourself and won't be wanting to bite your tongue off for speaking the truth;

it's a godsend, being dumb is. And here comes the general's cook, now what's he after?

Enter the cook and the chaplain.

THE CHAPLAIN: I have a message for you from your son Eilif, and the cook has come along because you made such a profound impression on him.

THE COOK: I just came along to get a bit of air.

MOTHER COURAGE: That you can always do here if you behave yourself, and if you don't I can deal with you. What does he want? I got no spare cash.

THE CHAPLAIN: Actually I had a message for his brother the paymaster.

MOTHER COURAGE: He ain't here now nor anywhere else neither. He ain't his brother's paymaster. He's not to lead him into temptation nor be clever at his expense. *Giving him money from the purse slung round her:* Give him this, it's a sin, he's banking on mother's love and ought to be ashamed of himself.

THE COOK: Not for long, he'll have to be moving off with the regiment, might be to his death. Give him a bit extra, you'll be sorry later. You women are tough, then later on you're sorry. A little glass of brandy wouldn't have been a problem, but it wasn't offered and, who knows, a bloke may lie beneath the green sod and none of you people will ever be able to dig him up again.

THE CHAPLAIN: Don't give way to your feelings, cook. To fall in battle is a blessing, not an inconvenience, and why? It is a war of faith. None of your common wars but a special one, fought for the faith and therefore pleasing to God.

THE COOK: Very true. It's a war all right in one sense, what with requisitioning, murder and looting and the odd bit of rape thrown in, but different from all the other wars because it's a war of faith; stands to reason. But it's thirsty work at that, you must admit.

THE CHAPLAIN *to Mother Courage, indicating the Cook*: I tried to stop him, but he says he's taken a shine to you, you figure in his dreams.

THE COOK *lighting a stumpy pipe*: Just want a glass of brandy from a fair hand, what harm in that? Only I'm groggy already cause the chaplain here's been telling such jokes all the way along you bet I'm still blushing.

MOTHER COURAGE: Him a clergyman too. I'd best give the pair of you a drink or you'll start making me immoral suggestions cause you've nowt else to do.

THE CHAPLAIN: Behold a temptation, said the court preacher, and fell. *Turning back to look at Kattrin as he leaves:* And who is this entrancing young person?

MOTHER COURAGE: That ain't an entrancing but a decent young person. *The chaplain and the cook go behind the cart with Mother Courage. Kattrin looks after them, then walks away from her washing towards the hat. She picks it up and sits down, pulling the red boots towards her. Mother Courage can be heard in the background talking politics with the chaplain and the cook.*

MOTHER COURAGE: Those Poles here in Poland had no business sticking their noses in. Right, our king moved in on them, horse and foot, but did they keep the peace? no, went and stuck their noses into their own affairs, they did, and fell on king just as he was quietly clearing off. They committed a breach of peace, that's what, so blood's on their own head.

THE CHAPLAIN: All our king minded about was freedom. The emperor had made slaves of them all, Poles and Germans alike, and the king had to liberate them.

THE COOK: Just what I say, your brandy's first rate, I weren't mistaken in your face, but talk of the king, it cost the king dear trying to give freedom to Germany, what with giving Sweden the salt tax, what cost the poor folk a bit, so I've heard, on top of which he had to have the Germans locked up and drawn and quartered cause they wanted to carry on slaving for the emperor. Course the king took a serious view when anybody didn't want to be free. He set out by just trying to protect Poland against bad people, particularly the emperor, then it started to become a habit till he ended up protecting the whole of Germany. They didn't half kick. So the poor old king's had nowt but trouble for all his kindness and expenses, and that's something he had to make up for by taxes of course, which caused bad blood, not that he'd let a little matter like that depress him. One thing he had on his side, God's word, that was a help. Because otherwise folk would of been saying he done it all for himself and to make a bit on the side. So he's always had a good conscience, which was the main point.

MOTHER COURAGE: Anyone can see you're no Swede or you wouldn't be talking that way about the Hero King.

THE CHAPLAIN: After all he provides the bread you eat.

THE COOK: I don't eat it, I bake it.

MOTHER COURAGE: They'll never beat him, and why, his men got faith in him. *Seriously:* To go by what the big shots say, they're waging war for almighty God and in the name of everything that's good and lovely. But look closer, they ain't so silly, they're waging it for what they can get. Else little folk like me wouldn't be in it at all.

THE COOK: That's the way it is.

THE CHAPLAIN: As a Dutchman you'd do better to glance at the flag above your head before venting your opinions here in Poland.

MOTHER COURAGE: All good Lutherans here. Prosit!

Kattrin has put on Yvette's hat and begun strutting around in imitation of her way of walking.

Suddenly there is a noise of cannon fire and shooting. Drums. Mother Courage, the Cook and the Chaplain rush out from behind the cart, the two last-named still carrying their glasses. The armourer and another soldier run up to the cannon and try to push it away.

MOTHER COURAGE: What's happening? Wait till I've taken my washing down, you louts! *She tries to rescue her washing.*

THE ARMOURER: The Catholics! Broken through. Don't know if we'll get out of here. *To the soldier:* Get that gun shifted! *Runs on.*

THE COOK: God, I must find the general. Courage, I'll drop by in a day or two for another talk.

MOTHER COURAGE: Wait, you forgot your pipe.

THE COOK *in the distance:* Keep it for me. I'll be needing it.

MOTHER COURAGE: Would happen just as we're making a bit of money.

THE CHAPLAIN: Ah well, I'll be going too. Indeed, if the enemy is so close as that it might be dangerous. Bléssed are the peacemakers is the motto in wartime. If only I had a cloak to cover me.

MOTHER COURAGE: I ain't lending no cloaks, not on your life. I been had too often.

THE CHAPLAIN: But my faith makes it particularly dangerous for me.

MOTHER COURAGE *gets him a cloak:* Goes against my conscience, this does. Now you run along.

THE CHAPLAIN: Thank you, dear lady, that's very generous of you, but I think it might be wiser for me to remain seated here; it could arouse suspicion and bring the enemy down on me if I were seen to run.

MOTHER COURAGE *to the soldier:* Leave it, you fool, who's going to pay you for that? I'll look after it for you, you're risking your neck.

THE SOLDIER *running away:* You can tell 'em I tried.

MOTHER COURAGE: Cross my heart. *Sees her daughter with the hat.* What you doing with that strumpet's hat? Take that lid off, you gone crazy? And the enemy arriving any minute! *Pulls the hat off Kattrin's head.* Want 'em to pick you up and make a prostitute of you? And she's gone and put those boots on, whore of Babylon! Off with those boots! *Tries to tug them off her.* Jesus Christ, chaplain, gimme a hand, get those boots off her, I'll be right back. *Runs to the cart.*

YVETTE *arrives, powdering her face*: Fancy that, the Catholics are coming. Where's my hat? Who's been kicking it around? I can't go about looking like this if the Catholics are coming. What'll they think of me? No mirror either. *To the chaplain*: How do I look? Too much powder?

THE CHAPLAIN: Exactly right.

YVETTE: And where are them red boots? *Fails to find them as Kattrin hides her feet under her skirt.* I left them here all right. Now I'll have to get to me tent barefoot. It's an outrage. *Exit.*

Swiss Cheese runs in carrying in a small box.

MOTHER COURAGE *arrives with her hands full of ashes. To Kattrin*: Here some ashes. *To Swiss Cheese*: What's that you're carrying?

SWISS CHEESE: Regimental cash box.

MOTHER COURAGE: Chuck it away. No more paymastering for you.

SWISS CHEESE: I'm responsible. *He goes to the rear.*

MOTHER COURAGE *to the chaplain*: Take your clerical togs off, padre, or they'll spot you under that cloak. *She rubs Kattrin's face with ash.* Keep still, will you? There you are, a bit of muck and you'll be safe. What a disaster. Sentries were drunk. Hide your light under a bushel, it says. Take a soldier, specially a Catholic one, add a clean face, and there's your instant whore. For weeks they get nowt to eat, then soon as they manage to get it by looting they're falling on anything in skirts. That ought to do. Let's have a look. Not bad. Looks like you been grubbing in muckheap. Stop trembling. Nothing'll happen to you like that. *To Swiss Cheese*: Where d'you leave cash box?

SWISS CHEESE: Thought I'd put it in cart.

MOTHER COURAGE *horrified*: What, my cart? Sheer criminal

idiocy. Only take me eyes off you one instant. Hang us all three, they will.

SWISS CHEESE: I'll put it somewhere else then, or clear out with it.

MOTHER COURAGE: You sit on it, it's too late now.

CHAPLAIN *who is changing his clothes downstage*: For heaven's sake, the flag!

MOTHER COURAGE *hauls down the regimental flag*: Bozhe moi! I'd given up noticing it were there. Twenty-five years I've had it.

The thunder of cannon intensifies.

A morning three days later. The cannon has gone. Mother Courage, Kattrin, the Chaplain and Swiss Cheese are sitting gloomily over a meal.

SWISS CHEESE: That's three days I been sitting around with nowt to do, and sergeant's always been kind to me but any moment now he'll start asking where's Swiss Cheese with the pay box?

MOTHER COURAGE: You thank your stars they ain't after you.

THE CHAPLAIN: What can I say? I can't even hold a service here, it might make trouble for me. Whosoever hath a full heart, his tongue runneth over, it says, but heaven help me if mine starts running over.

MOTHER COURAGE: That's how it goes. Here they sit, one with his faith and the other with his cash box. Dunno which is more dangerous.

THE CHAPLAIN: We are all of us in God's hands.

MOTHER COURAGE: Oh, I don't think it's as bad as that yet, though I must say I can't sleep nights. If it weren't for you, Swiss Cheese, things'd be easier. I think I got meself cleared. I told 'em I didn't hold with Antichrist, the Swedish one with horns on, and I'd observed left horn was a bit unserviceable. Half way through their interrogation I asked where I could get church candles not too dear. I knows the lingo cause Swiss Cheese's dad were Catholic, often used to make jokes about it, he did. They didn't believe me all that much, but they ain't got no regimental canteen lady. So they're winking an eye. Could turn out for the best, you know. We're prisoners, but same like fleas on dog.

THE CHAPLAIN: That's good milk. But we'll need to cut down our Swedish appetites a bit. After all, we've been defeated.

MOTHER COURAGE: Who's been defeated? Look, victory and defeat ain't bound to be same for the big shots up top as for them below, not by no means. Can be times the bottom lot find a defeat really pays them. Honour's lost, nowt else. I remember once up in Livonia our general took such a beating from enemy I got a horse off our baggage train in the confusion, pulled me cart seven months, he did, before we won and they checked up. As a rule you can say victory and defeat both come expensive to us ordinary folk. Best thing for us is when politics get bogged down solid. *To Swiss Cheese:* Eat up.

SWISS CHEESE: Got no appetite for it. What's sergeant to do when pay day comes round?

MOTHER COURAGE: They don't have pay days on a retreat.

SWISS CHEESE: It's their right, though. They needn't retreat if they don't get paid. Needn't stir a foot.

MOTHER COURAGE: Swiss Cheese, you're that conscientious it makes me quite nervous. I brought you up to be honest, you not being clever, but you got to know where to stop. Chaplain and me, we're off now to buy Catholic flag and some meat. Dunno anyone so good at sniffing meat, like sleepwalking it is, straight to target. I'd say he can pick out a good piece by the way his mouth starts watering. Well, thank goodness they're letting me go on trading. You don't ask tradespeople their faith but their prices. And Lutheran trousers keep cold out too.

THE CHAPLAIN: What did the mendicant say when he heard the Lutherans were going to turn everything in town and country topsy-turvy? 'They'll always need beggars'. *Mother Courage disappears into the cart.* So she's still worried about the cash box. So far they've taken us all for granted as part of the cart, but how long for?

SWISS CHEESE: I can get rid of it.

THE CHAPLAIN: That's almost more dangerous. Suppose you're seen. They have spies. Yesterday a fellow popped up out of the ditch in front of me just as I was relieving myself first thing. I was so scared I only just suppressed an ejaculatory prayer. That would have given me away all right. I think what they'd like best is to go sniffing people's excrement to see if they're Protestants. The spy was a little runt with a patch over one eye.

MOTHER COURAGE *clambering out of the cart with a basket*: What have I found, you shameless creature? *She holds up the red boots in triumph.* Yvette's red high-heeled boots! Coolly went and pinched them, she did. Cause you put it in her head she was an enchanting young person. *She lays them in the basket.* I'm giving them back. Stealing Yvette's boots! She's wrecking herself for money. That's understandable. But you'd do it for nothing, for pleasure. What did I tell you: you're to wait till it's peace. No soldiers for you. You're not to start exhibiting yourself till it's peacetime.

THE CHAPLAIN: I don't find she exhibits herself.

MOTHER COURAGE: Too much for my liking. Let her be like a stone in Dalecarlia, where there's nowt else, so folk say 'Can't see that cripple', that's how I'd lief have her. Then nowt'll happen to her. *To Swiss Cheese:* You leave that box where it is, d'you hear? And keep an eye on your sister, she needs it. The pair of you'll have me in grave yet. Sooner be minding a bagful of fleas.

She leaves with the Chaplain. Kattrin clears away the dishes.

SWISS CHEESE: Won't be able to sit out in the sun in shirt-

sleeves much longer. *Kattrin points at a tree.* Aye, leaves
turning yellow. *Kattrin asks by gestures if he wants a drink.*
Don't want no drink. I'm thinking. *Pause.* Said she can't
sleep. Best if I got rid of that box, found a good place for it.
All right, let's have a glass. *Kattrin goes behind the cart.* I'll
stuff it down the rat-hole by the river for the time being.
Probably pick it up tonight before first light and take it to
Regiment. How far can they have retreated in three days?
Bet sergeant's surprised. I'm agreeably disappointed in you,
Swiss Cheese, he'll say. I make you responsible for the
cash, and you go and bring it back.

*As Kattrin emerges from behind the cart with a full glass in her
hand, two men confront her. One is a sergeant, the other doffs his hat
to her. He has a patch over one eye.*

THE MAN WITH THE PATCH: God be with you, mistress.
Have you seen anyone round here from Second Finnish
Regimental Headquarters?

*Kattrin, badly frightened, runs downstage, spilling the brandy. The
two men look at one another, then withdraw on seeing Swiss Cheese
sitting there.*

SWISS CHEESE *interrupted in his thoughts*: You spilt half of it.
What are those faces for? Jabbed yourself in eye? I don't
get it. And I'll have have to be off, I've thought it over, it's
the only way. *He gets up. She does everything possible to make him
realise the danger. He only shrugs her off.* Wish I knew what
you're trying to say. Sure you mean well, poor creature,
just can't get words out. What's it matter your spilling my
brandy, I'll drink plenty more glasses yet, what's one more
or less? *He gets the box from the cart and takes it under his tunic.*
Be back in a moment. Don't hold me up now, or I'll be
angry. I know you mean well. Too bad you can't speak.

*As she tries to hold him back he kisses her and tears himself away.
Exit. She is desperate, running hither and thither uttering little
noises. The Chaplain and Mother Courage return. Kattrin rushes to
her mother.*

MOTHER COURAGE: What's all this? Pull yourself together, love. They done something to you? Where's Swiss Cheese? Tell it me step by step, Kattrin. Mother understands you. What, so that bastard did take the box? I'll wrap it round his ears, the little hypocrite. Take your time and don't gabble, use your hands, I don't like it when you howl like a dog, what'll his reverence say? Makes him uncomfortable. What, a one-eyed man came along?

THE CHAPLAIN: That one-eyed man is a spy. Have they arrested Swiss Cheese? *Kattrin shakes her head, shrugs her shoulders.* We're done for.

MOTHER COURAGE *fishes in her basket and brings out a Catholic flag, which the Chaplain fixes to the mast*: Better hoist new flag.

THE CHAPLAIN *bitterly*: All good Catholics here.

Voices are heard from the rear. The two men bring in Swiss Cheese.

SWISS CHEESE: Let me go, I got nowt. Don't twist my shoulder, I'm innocent.

SERGEANT: Here's where he came from. You know each other.

MOTHER COURAGE: Us? How?

SWISS CHEESE: I don't know her. Got no idea who she is, had nowt to do with them. I bought me dinner here, ten hellers it cost. You might have seen me sitting here, it was too salty.

SERGEANT: Who are you people, eh?

MOTHER COURAGE: We're law-abiding folk. That's right, he bought a dinner. Said it was too salty.

SERGEANT: Trying to pretend you don't know each other, that it?

MOTHER COURAGE: Why should I know him? Can't know everyone. I don't go asking 'em what they're called and are they a heretic; if he pays he ain't a heretic. You a heretic?

SWISS CHEESE: Go on.

THE CHAPLAIN: He sat there very properly, never opening his mouth except when eating. Then he had to.

SERGEANT: And who are you?

MOTHER COURAGE: He's just my potboy. Now I expect you gentlemen are thirsty, I'll get you a glass of brandy, you must be hot and tired with running.

SERGEANT: No brandy on duty. *To Swiss Cheese:* You were carrying something. Must have hidden it by the river. Was a bulge in your tunic when you left here.

MOTHER COURAGE: You sure it was him?

SWISS CHEESE: You must be thinking of someone else. I saw someone bounding off with a bulge in his tunic. I'm the wrong man.

MOTHER COURAGE: I'd say it was a misunderstanding too, such things happen. I'm a good judge of people, I'm Courage, you heard of me, everyone knows me, and I tell you that's an honest face he has.

SERGEANT: We're on the track of the Second Finnish Regiment's cash box. We got the description of the fellow responsible for it. Been trailing him two days. It's you.

SWISS CHEESE: It's not me.

SERGEANT: And you better cough it up, or you're a goner, you know. Where is it?

MOTHER COURAGE *urgently*: Of course he'd give it over rather than be a goner. Right out he'd say: I got it, here it is, you're too strong. He ain't all that stupid. Speak up, stupid idiot, here's the sergeant giving you a chance.

SWISS CHEESE: S'pose I ain't got it.

SERGEANT: Then come along. We'll get it out of you. *They lead him off.*

MOTHER COURAGE *calls after them*: He'd tell you. He's not that stupid. And don't you twist his shoulder! *Runs after them.*

Evening of the same day. The Chaplain and dumb Kattrin are cleaning glasses and polishing knives.

THE CHAPLAIN: Cases like that, where somebody gets caught, are not unknown in religious history. It reminds me of the Passion of Our Lord and Saviour. There's an old song about that. *He sings the Song of the Hours:*

> In the first hour Jesus mild
> Who had prayed since even
> Was betrayed and led before
> Pontius the heathen.

> Pilate found him innocent
> Free from fault and error
> Therefore, having washed his hands
> Sent him to King Herod.

> In the third hour he was scourged
> Stripped and clad in scarlet
> And a plaited crown of thorns
> Set upon his forehead.

> On the Son of Man they spat
> Mocked him and made merry.
> Then the cross of death was brought
> Given him to carry.

> At the sixth hour with two thieves
> To the cross they nailed him
> And the people and the thieves
> Mocked him and reviled him.

> This is Jesus King of Jews
> Cried they in derision
> Till the sun withdrew its light
> From that awful vision.

At the ninth hour Jesus wailed
Why hast thou me forsaken?
Soldiers brought him vinegar
Which he left untaken.

Then he yielded up the ghost
And the earth was shaken.
Rended was the temple's veil
And the saints were wakened.

Soldiers broke the two thieves' legs
As the night descended
Thrust a spear in Jesus' side
When his life had ended.

Still they mocked, as from his wound
Flowed the blood and water
And blasphemed the Son of Man
With their cruel laughter.*

MOTHER COURAGE *entering excitedly*: It's touch and go. They say sergeant's open to reason though. Only we mustn't let on it's Swiss Cheese else they'll say we helped him. It's a matter of money, that's all. But where's money to come from? Hasn't Yvette been round? I ran into her, she's got her hooks on some colonel, maybe he'd buy her a canteen business.

THE CHAPLAIN: Do you really wish to sell?

MOTHER COURAGE: Where's money for sergeant to come from?

THE CHAPLAIN: What'll you live on, then?

MOTHER COURAGE: That's just it.

Yvette Pottier arrives with an extremely ancient colonel.

YVETTE *embracing Mother Courage*: My dear Courage, fancy

* Song translated by Ralph Manheim

seeing you so soon. *Whispers:* He's not unwilling. *Aloud:* This is my good friend who advises me in business matters. I happened to hear you wanted to sell your cart on account of circumstances. I'll think it over.

MOTHER COURAGE: Pledge it, not sell, just not too much hurry, tain't every day you find a cart like this in wartime.

YVETTE *disappointed*: Oh, pledge. I though it was for sale. I'm not so sure I'm interested. *To the colonel:* How do you feel about it?

THE COLONEL: Just as you feel, pet.

MOTHER COURAGE: I'm only pledging it.

YVETTE: I thought you'd got to have the money.

MOTHER COURAGE *firmly*: I got to have it, but sooner run myself ragged looking for a bidder than sell outright. And why? The cart's our livelihood. It's a chance for you, Yvette; who knows when you'll get another like it and have a special friend to advise you, am I right?

YVETTE: Yes, my friend thinks I should clinch it, but I'm not sure. If it's only a pledge . . . so you agree we ought to buy outright?

THE COLONEL: I agree, pet.

MOTHER COURAGE: Best look and see if you can find anything for sale then; maybe you will if you don't rush it, take your friend along with you, say a week or fortnight, might find something suits you.

YVETTE: Then let's go looking. I adore going around looking for things, I adore going around with you, Poldi, it's such fun, isn't it? No matter if it takes a fortnight. How soon would you pay the money back if you got it?

MOTHER COURAGE: I'd pay back in two weeks, maybe one.

YVETTE: I can't make up my mind, Poldi chéri, you advise me. *Takes the colonel aside:* She's got to sell, I know, no problem there. And there's that ensign, you know, the fair-haired one, he'd be glad to lend me the money. He's crazy about me, says there's someone I remind him of. What do you advise?

THE COLONEL: You steer clear of him. He's no good. He's only making use of you. I said I'd buy you something, didn't I, pussykins?

YVETTE: I oughtn't to let you. Of course if you think the ensign might try to take advantage . . . Poldi, I'll accept it from you.

THE COLONEL: That's how I feel too.

YVETTE: Is that your advice?

THE COLONEL: That is my advice.

YVETTE *to Courage once more*: My friend's advice would be to accept. Make me out a receipt saying the cart's mine once two weeks are up, with all its contents, we'll check it now, I'll bring the two hundred florins later. *To the colonel:* You go back to the camp, I'll follow, I got to check it all and see there's nothing missing from my cart. *She kisses him. He leaves. She climbs up on the cart.* Not all that many boots, are there?

MOTHER COURAGE: Yvette, it's no time for checking your cart, s'posing it is yours. You promised you'd talk to sergeant about Swiss Cheese, there ain't a minute to lose, they say in an hour he'll be courtmartialled.

YVETTE: Just let me count the shirts.

MOTHER COURAGE *pulling her down by the skirt*: You bloody vampire. Swiss Cheese's life's at stake. And not a word about who's making the offer, for God's sake, pretend it's your friend, else we're all done for cause we looked after him.

YVETTE: I fixed to meet that one-eyed fellow in the copse, he should be there by now.

THE CHAPLAIN: It doesn't have to be the whole two hundred either, I'd go up to a hundred and fifty, that may be enough.

MOTHER COURAGE: Since when has it been your money? You kindly keep out of this. You'll get your hotpot all right, don't worry. Hurry up and don't haggle, it's life or death. *Pushes Yvette off.*

THE CHAPLAIN: Far be it from me to interfere, but what are we going to live on? You're saddled with a daughter who can't earn her keep.

MOTHER COURAGE: I'm counting on regimental cash box, Mr Clever. They'll allow it as his expenses.

THE CHAPLAIN: But will she get the message right?

MOTHER COURAGE: It's her interest I should spend her two hundred so she gets the cart. She's set on that, God knows how long that colonel of hers'll last. Kattrin, polish the knives, there's the pumice. And you, stop hanging round like Jesus on Mount of Olives, get moving, wash them glasses, we'll have fifty or more of cavalry in tonight and I don't want to hear a lot of 'I'm not accustomed to having to run about, oh my poor feet, we never ran in church'. Thank the Lord they're corruptible. After all, they ain't wolves, just humans out for money. Corruption in humans is same as compassion in God. Corruption's our only hope. Long as we have it there'll be lenient sentences and even an innocent man'll have a chance of being let off.

YVETTE *comes in panting*: They'll do it for two hundred. But it's got to be quick. Soon be out of their hands. Best thing is I go right away to my colonel with the one-eyed man. He's admitted he had the box, they put the thumbscrews on him. But he chucked it in the river soon as he saw they were on his track. The box is a write-off. I'll go and get the money from my colonel, shall I?

MOTHER COURAGE: Box is a write-off? How'm I to pay back two hundred then?

YVETTE: Oh, you thought you'd get it from the box, did you? And I was to be Joe Soap I suppose? Better not count on that. You'll have to pay up if you want Swiss Cheese back, or would you sooner I dropped the whole thing so's you can keep your cart?

MOTHER COURAGE: That's something I didn't allow for. Don't worry, you'll get your cart, I've said goodbye to it, had it seventeen years, I have. I just need a moment to think, it's bit sudden, what'm I to do, two hundred's too much for me, pity you didn't beat 'em down. Must keep a bit back, else any Tom, Dick and Harry'll be able to shove me in ditch. Go and tell them I'll pay hundred and twenty florins, else it's all off, either way I'm losing me cart.

YVETTE: They won't do it. That one-eyed man's impatient already, keeps looking over his shoulder, he's so worked up. Hadn't I best pay them the whole two hundred?

MOTHER COURAGE *in despair*: I can't pay that. Thirty years I been working. She's twenty-five already, and no husband. I got her to think of too. Don't push me, I know what I'm doing. Say a hundred and twenty, or it's off.

YVETTE: It's up to you. *Rushes off.*

Without looking at either the Chaplain or her daughter, Mother Courage sits down to help Kattrin polish knives.

MOTHER COURAGE: Don't smash them glasses, they ain't ours now. Watch what you're doing, you'll cut yourself. Swiss Cheese'll be back, I'll pay two hundred if it comes to the pinch. You'll get your brother, love. For eighty florins we could fill a pack with goods and start again. Plenty of folk has to make do.

THE CHAPLAIN: The Lord will provide, it says.

MOTHER COURAGE: See they're properly dry. *She cleans knives in silence. Kattrin suddenly runs behind the cart, sobbing.*

YVETTE *comes running in*: They won't do it. I told you so. The one-eyed man wanted to leave right away, said there was no point. He says he's just waiting for the drum-roll; that means sentence has been pronounced. I offered a hundred and fifty. He didn't even blink. I had to convince him to stay there so's I could have another word with you.

MOTHER COURAGE: Tell him I'll pay the two hundred. Hurry! *Yvette runs off. They sit in silence. The Chaplain has stopped polishing the glasses.* I reckon I bargained too long. *In the distance drumming is heard. The Chaplain gets up and goes to the rear. Mother Courage remains seated. It grows dark. The drumming stops. It grows light once more. Mother Courage is sitting exactly as before.*

YVETTE *arrives, very pale*: Well, you got what you asked for, with your haggling and trying to keep your cart. Eleven bullets they gave him, that's all. You don't deserve I should bother any more about you. But I did hear they don't believe the box really is in the river. They've an idea it's here and anyhow that you're connected with him. They're going to bring him here, see if you gives yourself away when you sees him. Thought I'd better warn you so's you don't recognise him, else you'll all be for it. They're right on my heels, best tell you quick. Shall I keep Kattrin away? *Mother Courage shakes her head.* Does she know? She mayn't have heard the drumming or know what it meant.

MOTHER COURAGE: She knows. Get her.

Yvette fetches Kattrin, who goes to her mother and stands beside her. Mother Courage takes her hand. Two lansequenets come carrying a stretcher with something lying on it covered by a sheet. The sergeant marches beside them. They set down the stretcher.

SERGEANT: Here's somebody we dunno the name of. It's got to be listed, though, so everything's shipshape. He had a meal here. Have a look, see if you know him. *He removes the sheet.* Know him? *Mother Courage shakes her head.* What, never see him before he had that meal here? *Mother Courage shakes her head.* Pick him up. Chuck him in the pit. He's got nobody knows him. *They carry him away.*

4

Mother Courage sings the Song of the Grand Capitulation

Outside an officer's tent.

Mother Courage is waiting. A clerk looks out of the tent.

THE CLERK: I know you. You had a paymaster from the Lutherans with you, what was in hiding. I'd not complain if I were you.

MOTHER COURAGE: But I got a complaint to make. I'm innocent, would look as how I'd a bad conscience if I let this pass. Slashed everything in me cart to pieces with their sabres, they did, then wanted I should pay five taler fine for nowt, I tell you, nowt.

CLERK: Take my tip, better shut up. We're short of canteens, so we let you go on trading, specially if you got a bad conscience and pay a fine now and then.

MOTHER COURAGE: I got a complaint.

CLERK: Have it your own way. Then you must wait till the captain's free. *Withdraws inside the tent.*

YOUNG SOLDIER *enters aggressively*: Bouque la Madonne! Where's that bleeding pig of a captain what's took my reward money to swig with his tarts? I'll do him.

OLDER SOLDIER *running after him*: Shut up. They'll put you in irons.

YOUNG SOLDIER: Out of there, you thief! I'll slice you into pork chops, I will. Pocketing my prize money after I'd swum the river, only one in the whole squadron, and now I can't even buy meself a beer. I'm not standing for that. Come on out there so I can cut you up!

OLDER SOLDIER: Blessed Mother of God, he's asking for trouble.

MOTHER COURAGE: Is it some reward he weren't paid?

YOUNG SOLDIER: Lemme go, I'll slash you too while I'm at it.

OLDER SOLDIER: He rescued the colonel's horse and got no reward for it. He's young yet, still wet behind the ears.

MOTHER COURAGE: Let him go, he ain't a dog you got to chain up. Wanting your reward is good sound sense. Why be a hero otherwise?

YOUNG SOLDIER: So's he can sit in there and booze. You're shit-scared, the lot of you. I done something special and I want my reward.

MOTHER COURAGE: Don't you shout at me, young fellow. Got me own worries, I have; any road you should spare your voice, be needing it when captain comes, else there he'll be and you too hoarse to make a sound, which'll make it hard for him to clap you in irons till you turn blue. People what shouts like that can't keep it up ever; half an hour, and they have to be rocked to sleep, they're so tired.

YOUNG SOLDIER: I ain't tired and to hell with sleep. I'm hungry. They make our bread from acorns and hemp-seed, and they even skimp on that. He's whoring away my reward and I'm hungry. I'll do him.

MOTHER COURAGE: Oh I see, you're hungry. Last year that general of yours ordered you all off roads and across fields so corn should be trampled flat; I could've got ten florins for a pair of boots s'pose I'd had boots and s'pose anyone'd been able to pay ten florins. Thought he'd be well away from that area this year, he did, but here he is, still there, and hunger is great. I see what you're angry about.

YOUNG SOLDIER: I won't have it, don't talk to me, it ain't fair and I'm not standing for that.

MOTHER COURAGE: And you're right; but how long? How long you not standing for unfairness? One hour, two hours? Didn't ask yourself that, did you, but it's the whole point, and why, once you're in irons it's too bad if you suddenly finds you can put up with unfairness after all.

YOUNG SOLDIER: What am I listening to you for, I'd like to know? Bouque la Madonne, where's that captain?

MOTHER COURAGE: You been listening to me because you knows it's like what I say, your anger has gone up in smoke already, it was just a short one and you needed a long one, but where you going to get it from?

YOUNG SOLDIER: Are you trying to tell me asking for my reward is wrong?

MOTHER COURAGE: Not a bit. I'm just telling you your anger ain't long enough, it's good for nowt, pity. If you'd a long one I'd be trying to prod you on. Cut him up, the swine, would be my advice to you in that case; but how about if you don't cut him up cause you feels your tail going between your legs? Then I'd look silly and captain'd take it out on me.

OLDER SOLDIER: You're perfectly right, he's just a bit crazy.

YOUNG SOLDIER: Very well, let's see if I don't cut him up. *Draws his sword.* When he arrives I'm going to cut him up.

CLERK *looks out*: The captain'll be here in one minute. Sit down.

The Young Soldier sits down.

MOTHER COURAGE: He's sitting now. See, what did I say? You're sitting now. Ah, how well they know us, no one need tell 'em how to go about it. Sit down! and, bingo, we're sitting. And sitting and sedition don't mix. Don't try to stand up, you won't stand the way you was standing before. I shouldn't worry about what I think; I'm no better, not one moment. Bought up all our fighting spirit, they have. Eh? S'pose I kick back, might be bad for business. Let me tell you a thing or two about the Grand Capitulation. *She sings the Song of the Grand Capitulation:*

Back when I was young, I was brought to realise
What a very special person I must be
(Not just any old cottager's daughter, what with my looks
    and my talents and my urge towards Higher Things)
And insisted that my soup should have no hairs in it.
No one makes a sucker out of me!
(All or nothing, only the best is good enough, each man for
    himself, nobody's telling *me* what to do.)
Then I heard a tit
Chirp: Wait a bit!
    And you'll be marching with the band
    In step, responding to command
    And striking up your little dance:
    Now we advance.
    And now: parade, form square!
    Then men swear God's there –
    Not the faintest chance!

In no time at all anyone who looked could see
That I'd learned to take my medicine with good grace.
(Two kids on my hands and look at the price of bread, and
    things they expect of you!)
When they finally came to feel that they were through with
    me
They'd got me grovelling on my face.
(Takes all sorts to make a world, you scratch my back and
    I'll scratch yours, no good banging your head against a
    brick wall.)
Then I heard that tit
Chirp: Wait a bit!
    And you'll be marching with the band
    In step, responding to command
    And striking up your little dance:
    Now they advance.
    And now: parade, form square!

Then men swear God's there –
Not the faintest chance!

I've known people tried to storm the summits:
There's no star too bright or seems too far away.
(Dogged does it, where there's a will there's a way, by hook
   or by crook.)
As each peak disclosed fresh peaks to come, it's
Strange how much a plain straw hat could weigh.
(You have to cut your coat according to your cloth.)
Then I hear the tit
Chirp: Wait a bit!
   And they'll be marching with the band
   In step, responding to command
   And striking up their little dance:
   Now they advance
   And now: parade, form square!
   Then men swear God's there –
   Not the faintest chance!

MOTHER COURAGE *to the young soldier*: That's why I reckon
you should stay there with your sword drawn if you're
truly set on it and your anger's big enough, because you got
grounds, I agree, but if your anger's a short one best leave
right away.

YOUNG SOLDIER: Oh stuff it. *He staggers off with the older
soldier following.*

CLERK *sticks his head out*: Captain's here now. You can make
your complaint.

MOTHER COURAGE: I changed me mind. I ain't complaining. *Exit.*

5

Two years have gone by. The war is spreading
to new areas. Ceaselessly on the move, Courage's
little cart crosses Poland, Moravia, Bavaria, Italy
then Bavaria again. 1631. Tilly's victory at
Magdeburg costs Mother Courage four officers'
shirts

Mother Courage's cart has stopped in a badly shot-up village.

*Thin military music in the distance. Two soldiers at the bar being
served by Kattrin and Mother Courage. One of them has a lady's fur
coat over his shoulders.*

MOTHER COURAGE: Can't pay, that it? No money, no
schnapps. They give us victory parades, but catch them
giving men their pay.
SOLDIER: I want my schnapps. I missed the looting. That
double-crossing general only allowed an hour's looting in
the town. He ain't an inhuman monster, he said. Town
must of paid him.
THE CHAPLAIN *stumbles in*: There are people still lying in
that yard. The peasant's family. Somebody give me a hand.
I need linen.
*The second soldier goes off with him. Kattrin becomes very excited
and tries to make her mother produce linen.*
MOTHER COURAGE: I got none. All my bandages was sold
to regiment. I ain't tearing up my officer's shirts for that
lot.
CHAPLAIN *calling back*: I need linen, I tell you.
MOTHER COURAGE *blocking Kattrin's way into the cart by*

sitting on the step: I'm giving nowt. They'll never pay, and why, nowt to pay with.

CHAPLAIN *bending over a woman he has carried in*: Why d'you stay around during the gunfire?

PEASANT WOMAN *feebly*: Farm.

MOTHER COURAGE: Catch them abandoning anything. But now I'm s'posed to foot the bill. I won't do it.

FIRST SOLDIER: Those are Protestants. What they have to be Protestants for?

MOTHER COURAGE: They ain't bothering about faith. They lost their farm.

SECOND SOLDIER: They're no Protestants. They're Catholics like us.

FIRST SOLDIER: No way of sorting 'em out in a bombardment.

A PEASANT *brought in by the chaplain*: My arm's gone.

THE CHAPLAIN: Where's that linen?

MOTHER COURAGE: I can't give nowt. What with expenses, taxes, loan interest and bribes. *Making guttural noises, Kattrin raises a plank and threatens her mother with it.* You gone plain crazy? Put that plank away or I'll paste you one, you cow. I'm giving nowt, don't want to, got to think of meself. *The Chaplain lifts her off the steps and sets her on the ground, then starts pulling out shirts and tearing them into strips.* My officers' shirts! Half a florin apiece! I'm ruined. *From the house comes the cry of a child in pain.*

THE PEASANT: The baby's in there still. *Kattrin dashes in.*

THE CHAPLAIN *to the woman*: Don't move. They'll get it out.

MOTHER COURAGE: Stop her, roof may fall in.

THE CHAPLAIN: I'm not going back in there.

MOTHER COURAGE *torn both ways*: Don't waste my precious linen.

Kattrin brings a baby out of the ruins.

MOTHER COURAGE: How nice, found another baby to cart around? Give it to its ma this instant, unless you'd have me fighting for hours to get it off you, like last time, d'you hear? *To the second soldier:* Don't stand there gawping, you go back and tell them cut out that music, we can see it's a victory with our own eyes. All your victories mean to me is losses.

THE CHAPLAIN *tying a bandage*: Blood's coming through. *Kattrin is rocking the baby and making lullaby noises.*

MOTHER COURAGE: Look at her, happy as a queen in all this misery; give it back at once, its mother's coming round. *She catches the first soldier, who has been attacking the drinks and is trying to make off with one of the bottles.* Psia krew! Thought you'd score another victory, you animal? Now pay.

FIRST SOLDIER: I got nowt.

MOTHER COURAGE *pulling the fur coat off his back*: Then leave that coat, it's stolen any road.

THE CHAPLAIN: There's still someone under there.

6

Outside the Bavarian town of Ingolstadt Courage participates in the funeral of the late Imperial commander Tilly. Discussions are held about war heroes and the war's duration. The Chaplain complains that his talents are lying fallow, and dumb Kattrin gets the red boots. The year is 1632

Inside a canteen tent.

It has a bar towards the rear. Rain. Sound of drums and Funeral music. The Chaplain and the regimental clerk are playing a board game. Mother Courage and her daughter are stocktaking.

THE CHAPLAIN: Now the funeral procession will be moving off.

MOTHER COURAGE: Too bad about commander in chief — twenty-two pairs those socks — he fell by accident, they say. Mist over fields, that was the trouble. General had just been haranguing a regiment saying they must fight to last man and last round, he was riding back when mist made him lose direction so he was up front and a bullet got him in midst of battle — only four hurricane lamps left. *A whistle from the rear. She goes to the bar.* You scrimshankers, dodging your commander in chief's funeral, scandal I call it. *Pours drinks.*

THE CLERK: They should never of paid troops out before the funeral. Instead of going now they're all getting pissed.

THE CHAPLAIN *to the clerk*: Aren't you supposed to go to the funeral?

THE CLERK: Dodged it cause of the rain.

MOTHER COURAGE: It's different with you, your uniform might get wet. I heard they wanted to toll bells for funeral as usual, except it turned out all churches had been blown to smithereens by his orders, so poor old commander in chief won't be hearing no bells as they let the coffin down. They're going to let off three salvoes instead to cheer things up — seventeen belts.

SHOUTS *from the bar*: Hey, Missis, a brandy!

MOTHER COURAGE: Let's see your money. No, I ain't having you in my tent with your disgusting boots. You can drink outside, rain or no rain. *To the clerk:* I'm only letting in sergeants and up. Commander in chief had been having his worries, they say. S'posed to have been trouble with Second Regiment cause he stopped their pay, said it was a war of faith and they should do it for free. *Funeral march. All look to the rear.*

THE CHAPLAIN: Now they'll be filing past the noble corpse.

MOTHER COURAGE: Can't help feeling sorry for those

generals and emperors, there they are maybe thinking
they're doing something extra special what folk'll talk about
in years to come, and earning a public monument, like
conquering the world for instance, that's a fine ambition for
a general, how's he to know any better? I mean, he plagues
hisself to death, then it all breaks down on account of
ordinary folk what just wants their beer and bit of a chat,
nowt higher. Finest plans get bolloxed up by the pettiness
of them as should be carrying them out, because emperors
can't do nowt themselves, they just counts on soldiers and
people to back 'em up whatever happens, am I right?

THE CHAPLAIN *laughs*: Courage, you're right, aside from the
soldiers. They do their best. Give me that lot outside there,
for instance, drinking their brandy in the rain, and I'd
guarantee to make you one war after another for a hundred
years if need be, and I'm no trained general.

MOTHER COURAGE: You don't think war might end, then?

THE CHAPLAIN: What, because the commander in chief's
gone? Don't be childish. They're two a penny, no shortage
of heroes.

MOTHER COURAGE: Ee, I'm not asking for fun of it, but
because I'm thinking whether to stock up, prices are low
now, but if war's going to end it's money down the drain.

THE CHAPLAIN: I realise it's a serious question. There've
always been people going round saying 'the war can't go on
for ever'. I tell you there's nothing to stop it going on for
ever. Of course there can be a bit of a breathing space. The
war may need to get its second wind, it may even have an
accident so to speak. There's no guarantee against that;
nothing's perfect on this earth of ours. A perfect war, the
sort you might say couldn't be improved on, that's something we shall probably never see. It can suddenly come to
a standstill for some quite unforeseen reason, you can't
allow for everything. A slight case of negligence, and it's
bogged down up to the axles. And then it's a matter of

hauling the war out of the mud again. But emperor and kings and popes will come to its rescue. So on the whole it has nothing serious to worry about, and will live to a ripe old age.

A SOLDIER *sings at the bar*:

> A schnapps, landlord, you're late!
> A soldier cannot wait
> To do his emperor's orders.

> Make it a double, this is a holiday.

MOTHER COURAGE: S'pose I went by what you say ...

THE CHAPLAIN: Think it out for yourself. What's to compete with the war?

THE SOLDIER *at the rear*:

> Your breast, my girl, you're late!
> A soldier cannot wait
> To ride across the borders.

THE CLERK *unexpectedly*: And what about peace? I'm from Bohemia and I'd like to go home some day.

THE CHAPLAIN: Would you indeed? Ah, peace. Where is the hole once the cheese has been eaten?

THE SOLDIER *at the rear*:

> Lead trumps, my friend, you're late!
> A soldier cannot wait.
> His emperor needs him badly.

> Your blessing, priest, you're late!
> A soldier cannot wait.
> Must lay his life down gladly.

THE CLERK: In the long run life's impossible if there's no peace.

THE CHAPLAIN: I'd say there's peace in war too; it has its peaceful moments. Because war satisfies all requirements, peaceable ones included, they're catered for, and it would simply fizzle out if they weren't. In war you can do a crap like in the depths of peacetime, then between one battle and the next you can have a beer, then even when you're moving up you can lay your head on your arms and have a bit of shuteye in the ditch, it's entirely possible. During a charge you can't play cards maybe, but nor can you in the depths of peacetime when you're ploughing, and after a victory there are various openings. You may get a leg blown off, then you start by making a lot of fuss as though it were serious, but afterwards you calm down or get given a schnapps, and you end up hopping around and the war's no worse off than before. And what's to stop you being fruitful and multi-plying in the middle of all the butchery, behind a barn or something, in the long run you can't be held back from it, and then the war will have your progeny and can use them to carry on with. No, the war will always find an outlet, mark my words. Why should it ever stop?

Kattrin has ceased working and is staring at the Chaplain.

MOTHER COURAGE: I'll buy fresh stock then. If you say so. *Kattrin suddenly flings a basket full of bottles to the ground and runs off.* Kattrin! *Laughs.* Damn me if she weren't waiting for peace. I promised her she'd get a husband soon as peace came. *Hurries after her.*

THE CLERK *standing up*: I won. You been talking too much. Pay up.

MOTHER COURAGE *returning with Kattrin*: Don't be silly, war'll go on a bit longer, and we'll make a bit more money, and peacetime'll be all the nicer for it. Now you go into town, that's ten minutes' walk at most, fetch things from Golden Lion, the expensive ones, we can fetch rest in cart later, it's all arranged, regimental clerk here will go with you. Nearly everybody's attending commander in chief's funeral, nowt can happen to you. Careful now, don't let them steal nowt, think of your dowry.

Kattrin puts a cloth over her head and leaves with the clerk.

THE CHAPLAIN: Is that all right to let her go with the clerk?

MOTHER COURAGE: She's not that pretty they'd want to ruin her.

THE CHAPLAIN: I admire the way you run your business and always win through. I see why they called you Courage.

MOTHER COURAGE: Poor folk got to have courage. Why, they're lost. Simply getting up in morning takes some doing in their situation. Or ploughing a field, and in a war at that. Mere fact they bring kids into world shows they got courage, cause there's no hope for them. They have to hang one another and slaughter one another, so just looking each other in face must call for courage. Being able to put up with emperor and pope shows supernatural courage, cause those two cost 'em their lives. *She sits down, takes a little pipe from her purse and smokes.* You might chop us a bit of kindling.

THE CHAPLAIN *reluctantly removing his coat and preparing to chop up sticks*: I happen to be a pastor of souls, not a wood-cutter.

MOTHER COURAGE: I got no soul, you see. Need firewood, though.

THE CHAPLAIN: Where's that stumpy pipe from?

MOTHER COURAGE: Just a pipe.

THE CHAPLAIN: What d'you mean, 'just', it's a quite particular pipe, that.

MOTHER COURAGE: Aha?

THE CHAPLAIN: That stumpy pipe belongs to the Oxen-stierna Regiment's cook.

MOTHER COURAGE: If you know that already why ask, Mr Clever?

THE CHAPLAIN: Because I didn't know if you were aware what you're smoking. You might just have been rummaging around in your things, come across some old pipe or other, and used it out of sheer absence of mind.

MOTHER COURAGE: And why not?

THE CHAPLAIN: Because you didn't. You're smoking that deliberately.

MOTHER COURAGE: And why shouldn't I?

THE CHAPLAIN: Courage, I'm warning you. It's my duty. Probably you'll never clap eyes on the gentleman again, and that's no loss but your good fortune. He didn't make at all a reliable impression on me. Quite the opposite.

MOTHER COURAGE: Really? Nice fellow that.

THE CHAPLAIN: So he's what you would call a nice fellow? I wouldn't. Far be it from me to bear him the least ill-will, but nice is not what I would call him. More like one of those Don Juans, a slippery one. Have a look at that pipe if you don't believe me. You must admit it tells you a good deal about his character.

MOTHER COURAGE: Nowt that I can see. Worn out, I'd call it.

THE CHAPLAIN: Practically bitten through, you mean. A man of wrath. That is the pipe of an unscrupulous man of wrath; you must see that if you have any discrimination left.

MOTHER COURAGE: Don't chop my chopping block in two.

THE CHAPLAIN: I told you I'm not a woodcutter by trade. I studied to be a pastor of souls. My talent and abilities are being abused in this place, by manual labour. My God-given endowments are denied expression. It's a sin. You have never heard me preach. One sermon of mine can put a regiment in such a frame of mind it'll treat the enemy like a flock of sheep. Life to them is a smelly old foot-cloth which they fling away in a vision of final victory. God has given me the gift of speech. I can preach so you'll lose all sense of sight and hearing.

MOTHER COURAGE: I don't wish to lose my sense of sight and hearing. Where'd that leave me?

THE CHAPLAIN: Courage, I have often thought that your

dry way of talking conceals more that just a warm heart. You too are human and need warmth.

MOTHER COURAGE: Best way for us to get this tent warm is have plenty of firewood.

THE CHAPLAIN: Don't change the subject. Seriously, Courage, I sometimes ask myself what it would be like if our relationship were to become somewhat closer. I mean, given that the whirlwind of war has so strangely whirled us together.

MOTHER COURAGE: I'd say it was close enough. I cook meals for you and you run around and chop firewood for instance.

THE CHAPLAIN *coming closer*: You know what I mean by closer; it's not a relationship founded on meals and wood-chopping and other such base necessities. Let your head speak, harden thyself not.

MOTHER COURAGE: Don't you come at me with that axe. That'd be too close a relationship.

THE CHAPLAIN: You shouldn't make a joke of it. I'm a serious person and I've thought about what I'm saying.

MOTHER COURAGE: Be sensible, padre. I like you. I don't want to row you. All I'm after is get myself and children through all this with my cart. I don't see it as mine, and I ain't in the mood for private affairs. Right now I'm taking a gamble, buying stores just when commander in chief's fallen and all the talk's of peace. Where d'you reckon you'd turn if I'm ruined? Don't know, do you? You chop us some kindling wood, then we can keep warm at night, that's quite something these times. What's this? *She gets up. Enter Kattrin, out of breath, with a wound above her eye. She is carrying a variety of stuff: parcels, leather goods, a drum and so on.*

MOTHER COURAGE: What happened, someone assault you? On way back? She was assaulted on her way back. Bet it was that trooper was getting drunk here. I shouldn't have let you go, love. Drop that stuff. Not too bad, just a flesh wound you got. I'll bandage it and in a week it'll be all right. Worse than wild beasts, they are. *She ties up the wound.*

THE CHAPLAIN: It's not them I blame. They never went raping back home. The fault lies with those that start wars, it brings humanity's lowest instincts to the surface.

MOTHER COURAGE: Calm down. Didn't clerk come back with you? That's because you're respectable, they don't bother. Wound ain't a deep one, won't leave no mark. There you are, all bandaged up. You'll get something, love, keep calm. Something I put aside for you, wait till you see. *She delves into a sack and brings out Yvette's red high-heeled boots.* Made you open your eyes, eh? Something you always wanted. They're yours. Put 'em on quick, before I change me mind. Won't leave no mark, and what if it does? Ones I'm really sorry for's the ones they fancy. Drag them around till they're worn out, they do. Those they don't care for they leaves alive. I seen girls before now had pretty faces, then in no time looking fit to frighten a hyaena. Can't even go behind a bush without risking trouble, horrible life they lead. Same like with trees, straight well-shaped ones get chopped down to make beams for houses and crooked ones live happily ever after. So it's a stroke of luck for you really. Them boots'll be all right, I greased them before putting them away.

Kattrin leaves the boots where they are and crawls into the cart.

THE CHAPLAIN: Let's hope she's not disfigured.

MOTHER COURAGE: She'll have a scar. No use her waiting for peacetime now.

THE CHAPLAIN: She didn't let them steal the things.

MOTHER COURAGE: Maybe I shouldn't have dinned that into her so. Wish I knew what went on in that head of hers. Just once she stayed out all night, once in all those years. Afterwards she went around like before, except she worked harder. Couldn't get her to tell what had happened. Worried me quite a while, that did. *She collects the articles brought by Kattrin, and sorts them angrily.* That's war for you. Nice way to get a living!

Sound of cannon fire.

THE CHAPLAIN: Now they'll be burying the commander in chief. This is a historic moment.

MOTHER COURAGE: What I call a historic moment is them bashing my daughter over the eye. She's half wrecked already, won't get no husband now, and her so crazy about kids; any road she's only dumb from war, soldier stuffed something in her mouth when she was little. As for Swiss Cheese I'll never see him again, and where Eilif is God alone knows. War be damned.

7

Mother Courage at the peak of her business career

High road.

The Chaplain, Mother Courage and Kattrin are pulling the cart, which is hung with new wares. Mother Courage is wearing a necklace of silver coins.

MOTHER COURAGE: I won't have you folk spoiling my war for me. I'm told it kills off the weak, but they're write-off in peacetime too. And war gives its people a better deal.

She sings:

And if you feel your forces fading
You won't be there to share the fruits.

But what is war but private trading
That deals in blood instead of boots?

And what's the use of settling down? Them as does are first to go. *Sings:*

Some people think to live by looting
The goods some others haven't got.
You think it's just a line they're shooting
Until you hear they have been shot.

And some I saw dig six feet under
In haste to lie down and pass out.
Now they're at rest perhaps they wonder
Just what was all their haste about.

They pull it further.

8

The same year sees the death of the Swedish king Gustavus Adolphus at the battle of Lützen. Peace threatens to ruin Mother Courage's business. Courage's dashing son performs one heroic deed too many and comes to a sticky end

Camp.

A summer morning. In front of the cart stand an old woman and her son. The son carries a large sack of bedding.

MOTHER COURAGE'S VOICE *from inside the cart*: Does it need to be this ungodly hour?

THE YOUNG MAN: We walked twenty miles in the night and got to be back today.

MOTHER COURAGE'S VOICE: What am I to do with bedding? Folk've got no houses.

THE YOUNG MAN: Best have a look first.

THE OLD WOMAN: This place is no good either. Come on.

THE YOUNG MAN: What, and have them sell the roof over our head for taxes? She might pay three florins if you throw in the bracelet. *Bells start ringing.* Listen, mother.

VOICES *from the rear*: Peace! Swedish king's been killed.

MOTHER COURAGE *sticks her head out of the cart. She has not yet done her hair*: What's that bell-ringing about in mid-week?

THE CHAPLAIN *crawling out from under the cart*: What are they shouting? Peace?

MOTHER COURAGE: Don't tell me peace has broken out just after I laid in new stock.

THE CHAPLAIN *calling to the rear*: That true? Peace?

VOICES: Three weeks ago, they say, only no one told us.

THE CHAPLAIN *to Courage*: What else would they be ringing the bells for?

VOICES: A whole lot of Lutherans have driven into town, they brought the news.

THE YOUNG MAN: Mother, it's peace. What's the matter? *The old woman has collapsed.*

MOTHER COURAGE *speaking into the cart*: Holy cow! Kattrin, peace! Put your black dress on, we're going to church. Least we can do for Swiss Cheese. Is it true, though?

THE YOUNG MAN: The people here say so. They've made peace. Can you get up? *The old woman stands up dumbfounded.* I'll get the saddlery going again, I promise. It'll all work out. Father will get his bedding back. Can you walk? *To the Chaplain:* She came over queer. It's the news. She never thought there'd be peace again. Father always said so. We're going straight home. *They go off.*

MOTHER COURAGE'S VOICE: Give her a schnapps.

THE CHAPLAIN: They've already gone.

MOTHER COURAGE'S VOICE: What's up in camp?

THE CHAPLAIN: They're assembling. I'll go on over. Shouldn't I put on my clerical garb?

MOTHER COURAGE'S VOICE: Best check up before parading yourself as heretic. I'm glad about peace, never mind if I'm ruined. Any road I'll have got two of me children through the war. Be seeing Eilif again now.

THE CHAPLAIN: And who's that walking down the lines? Bless me, the army commander's cook.

THE COOK *somewhat bedraggled and carrying a bundle*: What do I behold? The padre!

THE CHAPLAIN: Courage, we've got company.

Mother Courage clambers out.

THE COOK: I promised I'd drop over for a little talk soon as I had the time. I've not forgotten your brandy, Mrs Fierling.

MOTHER COURAGE: Good grief, the general's cook! After all these years! Where's my eldest boy Eilif?

THE COOK: Hasn't he got here? He left before me, he was on his way to see you too.

THE CHAPLAIN: I shall don my clerical garb, just a moment. *Goes off behind the cart.*

MOTHER COURAGE: Then he may be here any minute. *Calls into the cart:* Kattrin, Eilif's on his way. Get cook a glass of brandy, Kattrin! *Kattrin does not appear.* Drag your hair down over it, that's all right. Mr Lamb's no stranger. *Fetches the brandy herself.* She don't like to come out, peace means nowt to her. Took too long coming, it did. They gave her a crack over one eye, you barely notice it now but she thinks folks are staring at her.

THE COOK: Ah yes. War. *He and Mother Courage sit down.*

MOTHER COURAGE: Cooky, you caught me at bad moment. I'm ruined.

THE COOK: What? That's hard.

MOTHER COURAGE: Peace'll wring my neck. I went and took Chaplain's advice, laid in fresh stocks only t'other day. And now they're going to demobilise and I'll be left sitting on me wares.

THE COOK: What d'you want to go and listen to padre for? If I hadn't been in such a hurry that time, the Catholics arriving so quickly and all, I'd warned you against that man. All piss and wind, he is. So he's the authority around here, eh?

MOTHER COURAGE: He's been doing washing-up for me and helping pull.

THE COOK: Him pull! I bet he told you some of those jokes of his too, I know him, got a very unhealthy view of women, he has, all my good influence on him went for nowt. He ain't steady.

MOTHER COURAGE: You steady then?

THE COOK: Whatever else I ain't, I'm steady. Mud in your eye!

MOTHER COURAGE: Steady, that's nowt. I only had one steady fellow, thank God. Hardest I ever had to work in me life; he flogged the kids' blankets soon as autumn came, and he called me mouth-organ an unchristian instrument. Ask me, you ain't saying much for yourself admitting you're steady.

THE COOK: Still tough as nails, I see; but that's what I like about you.

MOTHER COURAGE: Now don't tell me you been dreaming of me nails.

THE COOK: Well, well, here we are, along with armistice bells and your brandy like what nobody else ever serves, it's famous, that is.

MOTHER COURAGE: I don't give two pins for your armistice bells just now. Can't see 'em handing out all the back pay what's owing, so where does that leave me with my famous brandy? Had your pay yet?

THE COOK *hesitantly*: Not exactly. That's why we all shoved off. If that's how it is, I thought, I'll go and visit friends. So here I am sitting with you.

MOTHER COURAGE: Other words you got nowt.

THE COOK: High time they stopped that bloody clanging. Wouldn't mind getting into some sort of trade. I'm fed up being cook to that lot. I'm s'posed to rustle them up meals out of tree roots and old bootsoles, then they fling the hot soup in my face. Cook these days is a dog's life. Sooner do war service, only of course it's peacetime now. *He sees the chaplain reappearing in his old garments*. More about that later.

THE CHAPLAIN: It's still all right, only had a few moths in it.

THE COOK: Can't see why you bother. You won't get your old job back, who are you to inspire now to earn his pay honourably and lay down his life? What's more I got a bone to pick with you, cause you advised this lady to buy a lot of unnecessary goods saying war would go on for ever.

THE CHAPLAIN *heatedly*: I'd like to know what concern that is of yours.

THE COOK: Because it's unscrupulous, that sort of thing is. How dare you meddle in other folks' business arrangements with your unwanted advice?

THE CHAPLAIN: Who's meddling? *To Courage:* I never knew this gentleman was such an intimate you had to account to him for everything.

MOTHER COURAGE: Keep your hair on, cook's only giving his personal opinion and you can't deny your war was a flop.

THE CHAPLAIN: You should not blaspheme against peace, Courage. You are a hyaena of the battlefield.

MOTHER COURAGE: I'm what?

THE COOK: If you're going to insult this lady you'll have to settle with me.

THE CHAPLAIN: It's not you I'm talking to. Your intentions are only too transparent. *To Courage:* But when I see you picking up peace betwixt your finger and your thumb like some dirty old snot-rag, then my humanity feels outraged; for then I see that you don't want peace but war, because you profit from it; in which case you shouldn't forget the ancient saying that whosoever sups with the devil needs a long spoon.

MOTHER COURAGE: I got no use for war, and war ain't got much use for me. But I'm not being called no hyaena, you and me's through.

THE CHAPLAIN: Then why grumble about peace when everybody's breathing sighs of relief? Because of some old junk in your cart?

MOTHER COURAGE: My goods ain't old junk but what I lives by, and you too up to now.

THE CHAPLAIN: Off war, in other words. Aha.

THE COOK *to the chaplain:* You're old enough to know it's always a mistake offering advice. *To Courage:* Way things are, your best bet's to get rid of certain goods quick as you can before prices hit rock-bottom. Dress yourself and get moving, not a moment to lose.

MOTHER COURAGE: That ain't bad advice. I'll do that, I guess.

THE CHAPLAIN: Because cooky says it.

MOTHER COURAGE: Why couldn't you say it? He's right, I'd best go off to market. *Goes inside the cart.*

THE COOK: That's one to me, padre. You got no presence of mind. What you should of said was: what, me offer advice, all I done was discuss politics. Better not take me on. Cock-fighting don't suit that get-up.

THE CHAPLAIN: If you don't stop your gob I'll murder you, get-up or no get-up.

THE COOK *pulling off his boots and unwrapping his foot-cloths:* Pity the war made such a godless shit of you, else you'd easily get another parsonage now it's peacetime. Cooks won't be needed, there's nowt to cook, but faith goes on just the same, nowt changed in that direction.

THE CHAPLAIN: Mr Lamb, I'm asking you not to elbow me out. Since I came down in the world I've become a better person. I couldn't preach to anyone now.

Enter Yvette Pottier in black, dressed up to the nines, carrying a cane. She is much older and fatter, and heavily powdered. She is followed by a manservant.

YVETTE: Hullo there, everybody. Is this Mother Courage's establishment?

THE CHAPLAIN: It is. And with whom have we the honour . . . ?

YVETTE: With the Countess Starhemberg, my good man. Where's Courage?

THE CHAPLAIN *calls into the cart*: The Countess Starhemberg wishes to speak to you.

MOTHER COURAGE'S VOICE: Just coming.

YVETTE: It's Yvette.

MOTHER COURAGE'S VOICE: Oh, Yvette!

YVETTE: Come to see how you are. *Sees the cook turn round aghast*: Pieter!

THE COOK: Yvette!

YVETTE: Well I never! How d'you come to be here?

THE COOK: Got a lift.

THE CHAPLAIN: You know each other then? Intimately?

YVETTE: I should think so. *She looks the cook over*. Fat.

THE COOK: Not all that skinny yourself.

YVETTE: All the same I'm glad to see you, you shit. Gives me a chance to say what I think of you.

THE CHAPLAIN: You say it, in full; but don't start till Courage is out here.

MOTHER COURAGE *coming out with all kinds of goods*: Yvette! *They embrace*. But what are you in mourning for?

YVETTE: Suits me, don't it? My husband the colonel died a few years back.

MOTHER COURAGE: That old fellow what nearly bought the cart?

YVETTE: His elder brother.

MOTHER COURAGE: Then you're sitting pretty. Nice to find somebody what's made it in this war.

YVETTE: Up and down and up again, that's the way it went.

MOTHER COURAGE: I'm not hearing a word against colonels, they make a mint of money.

THE CHAPLAIN: I would put my boots back on if I were you. *To Yvette:* You promised you would say what you think of the gentleman.

THE COOK: Don't kick up a stink here, Yvette.

MOTHER COURAGE: Yvette, this is a friend of mine.

YVETTE: That's old Puffing Piet.

THE COOK: Let's drop the nicknames. I'm called Lamb.

MOTHER COURAGE *laughs*: Puffing Piet! Him as made all the women crazy! Here, I been looking after your pipe for you.

THE CHAPLAIN: Smoking it, too.

YVETTE: What luck I can warn you against him. Worst of the lot, he was, rampaging along the whole Flanders coastline. Got more girls in trouble than he has fingers.

THE COOK: That's all a long while ago. Tain't true anyhow.

YVETTE: Stand up when a lady brings you into the conversation! How I loved this man! All the time he had a little dark girl with bandy legs, got her in trouble too of course.

THE COOK: Got you into high society more like, far as I can see.

YVETTE: Shut your trap, you pathetic remnant! Better watch out for him, though; fellows like that are still dangerous even when on their last legs.

MOTHER COURAGE *to Yvette*: Come along, got to get rid of my stuff afore prices start dropping. You might be able to put a word in for me at regiment, with your connections. *Calls into the cart:* Kattrin, church is off, I'm going to market instead. When Eilif turns up, one of you give him a drink. *Exit with Yvette.*

YVETTE *as she leaves*: Fancy a creature like that ever making me leave the straight and narrow path. Thank my lucky stars I managed to reach the top all the same. But I've cooked your goose, Puffing Piet, and that's something that'll be credited to me one day in the world to come.

THE CHAPLAIN: I would like to take as a text for our little talk 'The mills of God grind slowly'. Weren't you complaining about my jokes?

THE COOK: Dead out of luck, I am. It's like this, you see: I thought I might get a hot meal. Here am I starving, and now they'll be talking about me and she'll get quite a wrong picture. I think I'll clear out before she's back.

THE CHAPLAIN: I think so too.

THE COOK: Padre, I'm fed up already with this bloody peace. Human race has to go through fire and sword cause it's sinful from the cradle up. I wish I could be roasting a fat capon once again for the general, wherever he's got to, in mustard sauce with a carrot or two.

THE CHAPLAIN: Red cabbage. Red cabbage for a capon.

THE COOK: You're right, but carrots was what he had to have.

THE CHAPLAIN: No sense of what's fitting.

THE COOK: Not that it stopped you guzzling your share.

THE CHAPLAIN: With misgivings.

THE COOK: Anyway you must admit those were the days.

THE CHAPLAIN: I might admit it if pressed.

THE COOK: Now you've called her a hyaena your days here are finished. What you staring at?

THE CHAPLAIN: Eilif! *Eilif arrives, followed by soldiers with pikes. His hands are fettered. His face is chalky-white.* What's wrong?

EILIF: Where's mother?

THE CHAPLAIN: Gone into town.

EILIF: I heard she was around. They've allowed me to come and see her.

THE COOK *to the soldiers*: What you doing with him?

A SOLDIER: Something not nice.

THE CHAPLAIN: What's he been up to?

THE SOLDIER: Broke into a peasant's place. The wife's dead.

THE CHAPLAIN: How could you do a thing like that?

EILIF: It's what I did last time, ain't it?

THE COOK: Aye, but it's peace now.

EILIF: Shut up. All right if I sit down till she comes?

THE SOLDIER: We've no time.

THE CHAPLAIN: In wartime they recommended him for that, sat him at the general's right hand. Dashing, it was, in those days. Any chance of a word with the provost-marshal?

THE SOLDIER: Wouldn't do no good. Taking some peasant's cattle, what's dashing about that?

THE COOK: Dumb, I call it.

EILIF: If I'd been dumb you'd of starved, clever bugger.

THE COOK: But as you were clever you're going to be shot.

THE CHAPLAIN: We'd better fetch Kattrin out anyhow.

EILIF: Sooner have a glass of schnapps, could do with that.

THE SOLDIER: No time, come along.

THE CHAPLAIN: And what shall we tell your mother?

EILIF: Tell her it wasn't any different, tell her it was the same thing. Or tell her nowt. *The soldiers propel him away.*

THE CHAPLAIN: I'll accompany you on your grievous journey.

EILIF: Don't need any bloody parsons.

THE CHAPLAIN: Wait and see. *Follows him.*

THE COOK *calls after them*: I'll have to tell her, she'll want to see him.

THE CHAPLAIN: I wouldn't tell her anything. At most that

he was here and will come again, maybe tomorrow. By then I'll be back and can break it to her. *Hurries off.*

The cook looks after him, shaking his head, then walks restlessly around. Finally he comes up to the cart.

THE COOK: Hoy! Don't you want to come out? I can understand you hiding away from peace. Like to do the same myself. Remember me, I'm general's cook? I was wondering if you'd a bit of something to eat while I wait for your mum. I don't half feel like a bit of pork, or bread even, just to fill the time. *Peers inside.* Head under blanket. *Sound of gunfire off.*

MOTHER COURAGE *runs in, out of breath and with all her goods still*: Cooky, peacetime's over. War's been on again three days now. Heard news before selling me stuff, thank God. They're having a shooting match with Lutherans in town. We must get cart away at once. Kattrin, pack up! What you in the dumps for? What's wrong?

THE COOK: Nowt.

MOTHER COURAGE: Something is. I see it way you look.

THE COOK: Cause war's starting up again, I s'pose. Looks as if it'll be tomorrow night before I get next hot food inside me.

MOTHER COURAGE: You're lying, cooky.

THE COOK: Eilif was here. Had to leave almost at once, though.

MOTHER COURAGE: Was he now? Then we'll be seeing him on march. I'm joining our side this time. How's he look?

THE COOK: Same as usual.

MOTHER COURAGE: Oh, he'll never change. Take more than war to steal him from me. Clever, he is. You going to help me get packed? *Begins to pack up.* What's his news? Still in general's good books? Say anything about his deeds of valour?

THE COOK *glumly*: Repeated one of them, I'm told.

MOTHER COURAGE: Tell it me later, we got to move off. *Kattrin appears.* Kattrin, peacetime's finished now. We're moving on. *To the cook:* How about you?

THE COOK: Have to join up again.

MOTHER COURAGE: Why don't you . . . Where's padre?

THE COOK: Went into town with Eilif.

MOTHER COURAGE: Then you come along with us a way. Need somebody to help me.

THE COOK: That business with Yvette, you know. . .

MOTHER COURAGE: Done you no harm in my eyes. Opposite. Where there's smoke there's fire, they say. You coming along?

THE COOK: I won't say no.

MOTHER COURAGE: The Twelfth moved off already. Take the shaft. Here's a bit of bread. We must get round behind to Lutherans. Might even be seeing Eilif tonight. He's my favourite one. Short peace, wasn't it? Now we're off again. *She sings as the cook and Kattrin harness themselves up:*

From Ulm to Metz, from Metz to Munich
Courage will see the war gets fed.
The war will show a well-filled tunic
Given its daily shot of lead.
But lead alone can hardly nourish
It must have soldiers to subsist.
It's you it needs to make it flourish.
The war's still hungry. So enlist!

9

It is the seventeenth year of the great war of faith. Germany has lost more than half her inhabitants. Those who survive the bloodbath are killed off by terrible epidemics. Once fertile areas are ravaged by famine, wolves roam the burnt-out towns. In autumn 1634 we find Courage in the Fichtelgebirge, off the main axis of the Swedish armies. The winter this year is early and harsh. Business is bad, so that there is nothing to do but beg. The cook gets a letter from Utrecht and is sent packing

Outside a semi-dilapidated parsonage.

Grey morning in early winter. Gusts of wind. Mother Courage and the cook in shabby sheepskins, drawing the cart.

THE COOK: It's all dark, nobody up yet.

MOTHER COURAGE: Except it's parson's house. Have to crawl out of bed to ring bells. Then he'll have hot soup.

THE COOK: What from when whole village is burnt, we seen it.

MOTHER COURAGE: It's lived in, though, dog was barking.

THE COOK: S'pose parson's got, he'll give nowt.

MOTHER COURAGE: Maybe if we sing. . . .

THE COOK: I've had enough. *Abruptly:* Got a letter from Utrecht saying mother died of cholera and inn's mine. Here's letter if you don't believe me. No business of yours the way aunty goes on about my mode of existence, but have a look.

MOTHER COURAGE *reads the letter*: Lamb, I'm tired too of always being on the go. I feel like butcher's dog, dragging meat round customers and getting nowt off it. I got nowt left to sell, and folk got nowt left to buy nowt with. Saxony a fellow in rags tried landing me a stack of old books for two eggs, Württemberg they wanted to swap their plough for a titchy bag of salt. What's to plough for? Nowt growing no more, just brambles. In Pomerania villages are s'posed to have started in eating the younger kids, and nuns have been caught sticking folk up.

THE COOK: World's dying out.

MOTHER COURAGE: Sometimes I sees meself driving through hell with me cart selling brimstone, or across heaven with packed lunches for hungry souls. Give me my kids what's left, let's find some place they ain't shooting, and I'd like a few more years undisturbed.

THE COOK: You and me could get that inn going, Courage, think it over. Made up me mind in the night, I did: back to Utrecht with or without you, and starting today.

MOTHER COURAGE: Have to talk to Kattrin. That's a bit quick for me; I'm against making decisions all freezing cold and nowt inside you. Kattrin! *Kattrin climbs out of the cart.* Kattrin, got something to tell you. Cook and I want to go to Utrecht. He's been left an inn there. That'd be a settled place for you, let you meet a few people. Lots of 'em respect somebody mature, looks ain't everything. I'd like it too. I get on with cook. Say one thing for him, got a head for business. We'd have our meals for sure, not bad, eh? And your own bed too; like that, wouldn't you? Road's no life really. God knows how you might finish up. Lousy already, you are. Have to make up our minds, see, we could move with the Swedes, up north, they're somewhere up that way. *She points to the left.* Reckon that's fixed, Kattrin.

THE COOK: Anna, I got something private to say to you.

MOTHER COURAGE: Get back in cart, Kattrin.

Kattrin climbs back.

THE COOK: I had to interrupt, cause you don't understand, far as I can see. I didn't think there was need to say it, sticks out a mile. But if it don't, then let me tell you straight, no question of taking her along, not on your life. You get me, eh.

Kattrin sticks her head out of the cart behind them and listens.

MOTHER COURAGE: You mean I'm to leave Kattrin back here?

THE COOK: Use your imagination. Inn's got no room. It ain't one of the sort got three bar parlours. Put our backs in it we two'll get a living, but not three, no chance of that. She can keep cart.

MOTHER COURAGE: Thought she might find husband in Utrecht.

THE COOK: Go on, make me laugh. Find a husband, how? Dumb and that scar on top of it. And at her age?

MOTHER COURAGE: Don't talk so loud.

THE COOK: Loud or soft, no getting over facts. And that's another reason why I can't have her in the inn. Customers don't want to be looking at that all the time. Can't blame them.

MOTHER COURAGE: Shut your big mouth. I said not so loud.

THE COOK: Light's on in parson's house. We can try singing.

MOTHER COURAGE: Cooky, how's she to pull the cart on her own? War scares her. She'll never stand it. The dreams she must have... I hear her nights groaning. Mostly after a battle. What's she seeing in those dreams, I'd like to know. She's got a soft heart. Lately I found she'd got another hedgehog tucked away what we'd run over.

THE COOK: Inn's too small. *Calls out:* Ladies and gentlemen, domestic staff and other residents! We are now going to

give you a song concerning Solomon, Julius Caesar and
other famous personages what had bad luck. So's you can
see we're respectable folk, which makes it difficult to carry
on, particularly in winter.

They sing:

You saw sagacious Solomon
You know what came of him.
To him complexities seemed plain.
He cursed the hour that gave birth to him
And saw that everything was vain.
How great and wise was Solomon!
The world however didn't wait
But soon observed what followed on.
It's wisdom that had brought him to this state –
How fortunate the man with none!

Yes, the virtues are dangerous stuff in this world, as this
fine song proves, better not to have them and have a
pleasant life and breakfast instead, hot soup for instance.
Look at me: I haven't any but I'd like some. I'm a serving
soldier but what good did my courage do me in all them
battles, nowt, here I am starving and better have been shit-
scared and stayed at home. For why?

You saw courageous Caesar next
You know what he became.
They deified him in his life
Then had him murdered just the same.
And as they raised the fatal knife
How loud he cried: You too, my son!
The world however didn't wait
But soon observed what followed on.
It's courage that had brought him to that state.
How fortunate the man with none!

Sotto voce: Don't even look out. *Aloud:* Ladies and gentlemen, domestic staff and other inmates! All right, you may
say, gallantry never cooked a man's dinner, what about
trying honesty? You can eat all you want then, or anyhow
not stay sober. How about it?

> You heard of honest Socrates
> The man who never lied:
> They weren't so grateful as you'd think
> Instead the rulers fixed to have him tried
> And handed him the poisoned drink.
> How honest was the people's noble son!
> The world however didn't wait
> But soon observed what followed on.
> It's honesty that brought him to that state.
> How fortunate the man with none!

Ah yes, they say, be unselfish and share what you've got,
but how about if you got nowt? It's all very well to say
the do-gooders have a hard time, but you still got to have
something. Aye, unselfishness is a rare virtue, cause it just
don't pay.

> Saint Martin couldn't bear to see
> His fellows in distress.
> He met a poor man in the snow
> And shared his cloak with him, we know.
> Both of them therefore froze to death.
> His place in Heaven was surely won!
> The world however didn't wait
> But soon observed what followed on.
> Unselfishness had brought him to that state.
> How fortunate the man with none!

That's how it is with us. We're respectable folk, stick
together, don't steal, don't murder, don't burn places

down. And all the time you might say we're sinking lower and lower, and it's true what the song says, and soup is few and far between, and if we weren't like this but thieves and murderers I dare say we'd be eating our fill. For virtues aren't their own reward, only wickednesses are, that's how the world goes and it didn't ought to.

> Here you can see respectable folk
> Keeping to God's own laws.
> So far he hasn't taken heed.
> You who sit safe and warm indoors
> Help to relieve our bitter need!
> How virtuously we had begun!
> The world however didn't wait
> But soon observed what followed on.
> It's fear of God that brought us to that state.
> How fortunate the man with none!

VOICE *from above*: Hey, you there! Come on up! There's hot soup if you want.

MOTHER COURAGE: Lamb, me stomach won't stand nowt. 'Tain't that it ain't sensible, what you say, but is that your last word? We got on all right.

THE COOK: Last word. Think it over.

MOTHER COURAGE: I've nowt to think. I'm not leaving her here.

THE COOK: That's proper senseless, nothing I can do about it though. I'm not a brute, just the inn's a small one. So now we better get on up, or there'll be nowt here either and wasted time singing in the cold.

MOTHER COURAGE: I'll get Kattrin.

THE COOK: Better bring a bit back for her. Scare them if they sees three of us coming. *Exeunt both.*

Kattrin climbs out of the cart with a bundle. She looks around to see if the other two have gone. Then she takes an old pair of trousers of the cook's and a skirt of her mother's, and lays them side by side on one of the wheels, so that they are easily seen. She has finished and is picking up her bundle to go, when Mother Courage comes back from the house.

MOTHER COURAGE *with a plate of soup*: Kattrin! Will you stop there? Kattrin! Where you off to with that bundle? Has devil himself taken you over? *She examines the bundle.* She's packed her things. You been listening? I told him nowt doing, Utrecht, his rotten inn, what'd we be up to there? You and me, inn's no place for us. Still plenty to be got out of war. *She sees the trousers and the skirt.* You're plain stupid. S'pose I'd seen that, and you gone away? *She holds Kattrin back as she tries to break away.* Don't you start thinking it's on your account I given him the push. It was cart, that's it. Catch me leaving my cart I'm used to, it ain't you, it's for cart. We'll go off in t'other direction, and we'll throw cook's stuff out so he finds it, silly man. *She climbs in and throws out a few other articles in the direction of the trousers.* There, he's out of our business now, and I ain't having nobody else in, ever. You and me'll carry on now. This winter will pass, same as all the others. Get hitched up, it looks like snow.

They both harness themselves to the cart, then wheel it round and drag it off. When the cook arrives he looks blankly at his kit.

10

During the whole of 1635 Mother Courage and her daughter Kattrin travel over the highroads of central Germany, in the wake of the increasingly bedraggled armies

High road.

Mother Courage and Kattrin are pulling the cart. They pass a peasant's house inside which there is a voice singing.

THE VOICE:
> The roses in our arbour
> Delight us with their show:
> They have such lovely flowers
> Repaying all our labour
> After the summer showers.
> Happy are those with gardens now:
> They have such lovely flowers.
>
> When winter winds are freezing
> As through the woods they blow
> Our home is warm and pleasing.
> We fixed the thatch above it
> With straw and moss we wove it.
> Happy are those with shelter now
> When winter winds are freezing.

Mother Courage and Kattrin pause to listen, then continue pulling.

11

January 1636. The emperor's troops are threatening the Protestant town of Halle. The stone begins to speak. Mother Courage loses her daughter and trudges on alone. The war is a long way from being over

The cart is standing, much the worse for wear, alongside a peasant's house with a huge thatched roof, backing on a wall of rock. It is night.

An ensign and three soldiers in heavy armour step out of the wood.

THE ENSIGN: I want no noise now. Anyone shouts, shove your pike into him.

FIRST SOLDIER: Have to knock them up, though, if we're to find a guide.

THE ENSIGN: Knocking sounds natural. Could be a cow bumping the stable wall.
   The soldiers knock on the door of the house. The peasant's wife opens it. They stop her mouth. Two soldiers go in.

MAN'S VOICE *within*: What is it?
   The soldiers bring out the peasant and his son.

THE ENSIGN *pointing at the cart, where Kattrin's head has appeared*: There's another one. *A soldier drags her out.* Anyone else live here beside you lot?

THE PEASANTS: This is our son. And she's dumb. Her mother's gone into town to buy stuff. For their business, cause so many people's getting out and selling things cheap. They're just passing through. Canteen folk.

THE ENSIGN: I'm warning you, keep quiet, or if there's the least noise you get a pike across your nut. Now I want someone to come with us and show us the path to the town. *Points to the young peasant.* Here, you.

THE YOUNG PEASANT: I don't know no path.

SECOND SOLDIER *grinning*: He don't know no path.

THE YOUNG PEASANT: I ain't helping Catholics.

THE ENSIGN *to the second soldier*: Stick your pike in his ribs.

THE YOUNG PEASANT *forced to his knees, with the pike threatening him*: I won't do it, not to save my life.

FIRST SOLDIER: I know what'll change his mind. *Goes towards the stable.* Two cows and an ox. Listen, you: if you're not reasonable I'll chop up your cattle.

THE YOUNG PEASANT: No, not that!

THE PEASANT'S WIFE *weeps*: Please spare our cattle, captain, it'd be starving us to death.

THE ENSIGN: They're dead if he goes on being obstinate.

FIRST SOLDIER: I'm taking the ox first.

THE YOUNG PEASANT *to his father*: Have I got to? *The wife nods.* Right.

THE PEASANT'S WIFE: And thank you kindly, captain, for sparing us, for ever and ever, Amen.

The peasant stops his wife from further expressions of gratitude.

FIRST SOLDIER: I knew the ox was what they minded about most, was I right?

Guided by the young peasant, the ensign and his men continue on their way.

THE PEASANT: What are they up to, I'd like to know. Nowt good.

THE PEASANT'S WIFE: Perhaps they're just scouting. What you doing?

THE PEASANT *putting a ladder against the roof and climbing up it*: Seeing if they're on their own. *From the top:* Something moving in the wood. Can see something down by the quarry. And there are men in armour in the clearing. And a gun. That's at least a regiment. God's mercy on the town and everyone in it!

THE PEASANT'S WIFE: Any lights in the town?

THE PEASANT: No. They'll all be asleep. *Climbs down.* If those people get in they'll butcher the lot.

THE PEASANT'S WIFE: Sentries're bound to spot them first.

THE PEASANT: Sentry in the tower up the hill must have been killed, or he'd have blown his bugle.

THE PEASANT'S WIFE: If only there were more of us.

THE PEASANT: Just you and me and that cripple.

THE PEASANT'S WIFE: Nowt we can do, you'd say. . . .

THE PEASANT: Nowt.

THE PEASANT'S WIFE: Can't possibly run down there in the blackness.

THE PEASANT: Whole hillside's crawling with 'em. We could give a signal.

THE PEASANT'S WIFE: What, and have them butcher us too?

THE PEASANT: You're right, nowt we can do.

THE PEASANT'S WIFE *to Kattrin*: Pray, poor creature, pray! Nowt we can do to stop bloodshed. You can't talk, maybe, but at least you can pray. He'll hear you if no one else can. I'll help you. *All kneel, Kattrin behind the two peasants.* Our Father, which art in Heaven, hear Thou our prayer, let not the town be destroyed with all what's in it sound asleep and suspecting nowt. Arouse Thou them that they may get up and go to the walls and see how the enemy approacheth with pikes and guns in the blackness across fields below the slope. *Turning to Kattrin:* Guard Thou our mother and ensure that the watchman sleepeth not but wakes up, or it will be too late. Succour our brother-in-law also, he is inside there with his four children, spare Thou them, they are innocent and know nowt. *To Kattrin, who gives a groan:* One of them's not two yet, the eldest's seven. *Kattrin stands up distractedly.* Our Father, hear us, for only Thou canst help; we look to be doomed, for why, we are weak and have no pike and nowt and can risk nowt and are in Thy hand along with our cattle and all the farm, and same with the town, it too is in Thy hand and the enemy is before the walls in great strength.

Unobserved, Kattrin has slipped away to the cart and taken from it something which she hides beneath her apron; then she climbs up the ladder on to the stable roof.

THE PEASANT'S WIFE: Forget not the children, what are in danger, the littlest ones especially, the old folk what can't move, and every living creature.

THE PEASANT: And forgive us our trespasses as we forgive them that trespass against us. Amen.

Sitting on the roof, Kattrin begins to beat the drum which she has pulled out from under her apron.

THE PEASANT'S WIFE: Jesus Christ, what's she doing?

THE PEASANT: She's out of her mind.

THE PEASANT'S WIFE: Quick, get her down.

The peasant hurries to the ladder, but Kattrin pulls it up on to the roof.

THE PEASANT'S WIFE: She'll do us in.

THE PEASANT: Stop drumming at once, you cripple!

THE PEASANT'S WIFE: Bringing the Catholics down on us!

THE PEASANT *looking for stones to throw*: I'll stone you.

THE PEASANT'S WIFE: Where's your feelings? Where's your heart? We're done for if they come down on us. Slit our throats, they will. *Kattrin stares into the distance towards the town and carries on drumming.*

THE PEASANT'S WIFE *to her husband*: I told you we shouldn't have allowed those vagabonds on to farm. What do they care if our last cows are taken?

THE ENSIGN *runs in with his soldiers and the young peasant*: I'll cut you to ribbons, all of you!

THE PEASANT'S WIFE: Please, sir, it's not our fault, we couldn't help it. It was her sneaked up there. A foreigner.

THE ENSIGN: Where's the ladder?

THE PEASANT: There.

THE ENSIGN *calls up*: I order you, throw that drum down. *Kattrin goes on drumming.*

THE ENSIGN: You're all in this together. It'll be the end of you.

THE PEASANT: They been cutting pine trees in that wood. How about if we got one of the trunks and poked her off. . . .

FIRST SOLDIER *to the ensign*: Permission to make a suggestion, sir! *He whispers something in the ensign's ear.* Listen, we got a suggestion could help you. Get down off there and come into town with us right away. Show us which your mother is and we'll see she ain't harmed. *Kattrin goes on drumming.*

THE ENSIGN *pushes him roughly aside*: She doesn't trust you; with a mug like yours it's not surprising. *Calls up:* Suppose I gave you my word? I can give my word of honour as an officer. *Kattrin drums harder.*

THE ENSIGN: Is nothing sacred to her?

THE YOUNG PEASANT: There's more than her mother involved, sir.

FIRST SOLDIER: This can't go on much longer. They're bound to hear in the town.

THE ENSIGN: We'll have somehow to make a noise that's louder than her drumming. What can we make a noise with?

FIRST SOLDIER: Thought we weren't s'posed to make no noise.

THE ENSIGN: A harmless one, you fool. A peaceful one.

THE PEASANT: I could chop wood with my axe.

THE ENSIGN: Good: you chop. *The peasant fetches his axe and attacks a tree-trunk.* Chop harder! Harder! You're chopping for your life. *Kattrin has been listening, drumming less loudly the while. She now looks wildly round, and goes on drumming.*

THE ENSIGN: Not loud enough. *To the first soldier:* You chop too.

THE PEASANT: Only got the one axe. *Stops chopping.*

THE ENSIGN: We'll have to set the farm on fire. Smoke her out, that's it.

THE PEASANT: It wouldn't help, captain. If the townspeople see a fire here they'll know what's up.

Kattrin has again been listening as she drums. At this point she laughs.

THE ENSIGN: Look at her laughing at us. I'm not having that. I'll shoot her down, and damn the consequences. Fetch the harquebus.

Three soldiers hurry off. Kattrin goes on drumming.

THE PEASANT'S WIFE: I got it, captain. That's their cart. If we smash it up she'll stop. Cart's all they got.

THE ENSIGN *to the young peasant:* Smash it up. *Calls up:* We're going to smash up your cart if you don't stop drumming. *The young peasant gives the cart a few feeble blows.*

THE PEASANT'S WIFE: Stop it, you animal!

Desperately looking towards the cart, Kattrin emits pitiful noises. But she goes on drumming.

THE ENSIGN: Where are those clodhoppers with the harquebus?

FIRST SOLDIER: Can't have heard nowt in town yet, else we'd be hearing their guns.

THE ENSIGN *calls up:* They can't hear you at all. And now we're going to shoot you down. For the last time: throw down that drum!

THE YOUNG PEASANT *suddenly flings away his plank:* Go on drumming! Or they'll all be killed! Go on, go on. . . .

The soldier knocks him down and beats him with his pike. Kattrin starts to cry, but she goes on drumming.

THE PEASANT'S WIFE: Don't strike his back! For God's sake, you're beating him to death!

The soldiers hurry in with the arquebus.

SECOND SOLDIER: Colonel's frothing at the mouth, sir. We're all for court-martial.

THE ENSIGN: Set it up! Set it up! *Calls up while the gun is being erected:* For the very last time: stop drumming! *Kattrin, in tears, drums as loud as she can.* Fire! *The soldiers fire. Kattrin is hit, gives a few more drumbeats and then slowly crumples.*

THE ENSIGN: That's the end of that.

But Kattrin's last drumbeats are taken up by the town's cannon. In the distance can be heard a confused noise of tocsins and gunfire.

FIRST SOLDIER: She's made it.

12

Before first light. Sound of the fifes and drums of troops marching off into the distance

In front of the cart Mother Courage is squatting by her daughter. The peasant family are standing near her.

THE PEASANTS *with hostility*: You must go, missis. There's only one more regiment behind that one. You can't go on your own.

MOTHER COURAGE: I think she's going to sleep. *She sings:*

> Lullaby baby
> What's that in the hay?
> Neighbours' kids grizzle
> But my kids are gay.
> Neighbours' are in tatters
> And you're dressed in lawn
> Cut down from the raiment an

Angel has worn.
Neighbours' kids go hungry
And you shall eat cake
Suppose it's too crumbly
You've only to speak.
Lullaby baby
What's that in the hay?
The one lies in Poland
The other – who can say?

Better if you'd not told her nowt about your brother-in-law's kids.

THE PEASANT: If you'd not gone into town to get your cut it might never of happened.

MOTHER COURAGE: Now she's asleep.

THE PEASANT'S WIFE: She ain't asleep. Can't you see she's passed over?

THE PEASANT: And it's high time you got away yourself. There are wolves around and, what's worse, marauders.

MOTHER COURAGE: Aye.

She goes and gets a tarpaulin to cover the dead girl with.

THE PEASANT'S WIFE: Ain't you got nobody else? What you could go to?

MOTHER COURAGE: Aye, one left. Eilif.

THE PEASANT *as Mother Courage covers the dead girl*: Best look for him, then. We'll mind her, see she gets proper burial. Don't you worry about that.

MOTHER COURAGE: Here's money for expenses.

She counts out coins into the peasant's hands.

The peasant and his son shake hands with her and carry Kattrin away.

THE PEASANT'S WIFE *as she leaves*: I'd hurry.

MOTHER COURAGE *harnessing herself to the cart*: Hope I can pull cart all right by meself. Be all right, nowt much inside it. Got to get back in business again.

Another regiment with its fifes and drums marches past in the background.

MOTHER COURAGE *tugging the cart*: Take me along!
Singing is heard from offstage:

With all its luck and all its danger
The war is dragging on a bit
Another hundred years or longer
The common man won't benefit.
Filthy his food, no soap to shave him
The regiment steals half his pay.
But still a miracle may save him:
Tomorrow is another day!
   The new year's come. The watchmen shout.
   The thaw sets in. The dead remain.
   Wherever life has not died out
   It staggers to its feet again.

Notes

(These notes are intended for use by overseas students as well as by English-born readers.)

Scene 1

3   *Spring 1624* — the play opens during the truce in the Polish-Swedish War (1622-1629) in the peaceful province of Dalecarlia in Central Sweden (see map) where fresh troops are being enlisted for the resumption of hostilities.

3   *canteen woman* — freelance camp-follower with a waggon from which she provides the troops with food, drink, clothing and sundry other items.

3   *recruiter* — soldier whose task was to find able-bodied young men in the civilian population and persuade them to join the army.

3   *four companies* — a company was a unit with 300 men.

4   *it stands to reason; no order, no war* — the discussion of the inter-dependence of war and order is comic here, but becomes grimly ironic in the light of the action that follows. Right-wing parties commonly have a 'law and order' lobby, and one of the claims made by Hitler and the Nazis was that they would restore order after the democratic shambles, as they would have put it, of the Weimar Republic.

4   *jew's-harp* — small musical instrument which you hold against your teeth while twanging the metal tongue with your finger.

4   *infanteers* — a deliberately archaic word for foot soldiers.

5   *While you command them into hell* — Courage's unconcerned zest for fattening soldiers for the slaughter is even clearer in the German version, which translates literally as: 'Once they're full, you have my blessing/to lead them into the jaws of hell'.

5   *Second Finnish Regiment* — Finland was under Swedish rule, so this regiment is part of the Swedish army.

5   *bombardment of Riga* — Riga was the capital of Livonia (see map), a Polish protectorate on the Baltic Sea. The Swedes besieged it in 1621 in the Polish-Swedish War.

5   *Altötting in Bavaria . . . Moravia* — to reach this small town on the Austrian border, or Moravia (see map), the war would have to travel 1000 miles from where Courage is. It eventually did just that, leaving devastation in its wake.

5   *florins* — the florin was a silver coin in 17th-century Germany (see note on p.13).

5   *licence* — trading in certain items, such as liquor, required then, as it does now, a licence from the authorities, in this case from the military.

6   *Eilif Nojocki* — Courage mocks the Sergeant with the complex paternity of her children. Nojocki is a Finnish name, but the 'father' Eilif remembers was French. Swiss Cheese had a Swiss father but is called Fejos after a Hungarian whose character, to compound the confusion, he has 'inherited'. Kattrin is half German, which tells us nothing at all about her father. This jaunty catalogue of miscegenation could be a dig at Nazi race theories; it bears out Courage's statement that she and her cart have seen the world.

7   *Jacob Ox and Esau Ox* — Jacob and Esau are brothers in the Bible.

8   *He's a chicken* — Courage denies the obvious, since Eilif is strong enough to haul the waggon; she does so to fend off the attention of the recruiter who is on the look-out for able-bodied men.

9   *She's got second sight* — she can foretell the future, as the soldiers would readily believe because she looks like a gypsy.

10   *all holy-holy* — joyless and puritanical, as might be expected of Protestants. Sweden is a Protestant country at war with Catholic Poland.

10   *no vale of joys* — ironic variation on the biblical image of life as a 'vale (or valley) of tears'.

10   *Oh, wretched mother* — the fortune-telling episode is farcical, and the audience realises that it is rigged. Courage's mock rhetoric at this point takes the audience into collusion with her, whereas the victims of her trick are too close to the dangers of war to treat it as a joke.

12   *bounty money* — money, in this case ten florins, offered as an inducement to join the army. The British equivalent was the 'King's shilling'. Once this money is accepted the recruit cannot leave the army, unless he deserts.

13   *Burnt child* — 'a burnt child fears the fire', says the proverb. Courage means that she has been cheated before.

13   *Wallhof* — a fortified town south east of Riga (see map). The

Polish-Swedish War had restarted in 1625, and the Swedish King
Gustavus Adolphus's victory at Wallhof in 1626 sealed his conquest
of Livonia.

Scene 2

13 *Sixty hellers* — a heller was a small coin, usually worth half a
pfennig. There were 240, 480 or 504 hellers to the florin at
different times and places in 17th-century Germany. Brecht seems
to be assuming that there are 100.

14 *We're conducting the siege* — as the cook rightly observes, it is
the Poles who are surrounded inside Wallhof, while the Swedes are
outside doing the besieging, but Courage's remark that the
countryside has been stripped of all food may well be accurate,
even though she is using this as an argument to force up the price
of her capon. In bargaining with the cook, Courage has met her
match. He too is a campaign-hardened professional, and both of
them enjoy haggling. In Brecht's first production the actor Bildt
underlined the cook's extrovert professionalism by making the
dressing of the capon later in the scene an elegant demonstration
of culinary skill.

15 *war of religion* — in the Polish-Swedish War Gustavus
Adolphus was fighting to establish Swedish control of the Baltic
provinces and to put an end to Catholic, Polish claims to the
throne of Sweden, which was Protestant, so he was already
championing Protestantism, as he was later to do in the Thirty
Years War. The General's Christianity, however, as his racy
comments on the peasants and the Chaplain show, is little more
than a licence to plunder the Catholic population.

15 *Falernian* — red wine from the district of Falerno in Italy.

16 *true faith* — carrying out the true faith, as opposed to
preaching it like the Chaplain, is equated here with tricking and
killing four peasants in cold blood.

17 *Necessity's the mother of invention* — the German version of
this proverb is 'times of need observe no commandments'. The
Chaplain is forced to concede that Christ's commandment to
'love thy neighbour as thy self' may not apply in time of war when
people are hungry. The General then rewards him with a glass of
wine for twisting the Gospel to suit him.

17 *Pharisee* — hypocrite (from the Bible).

18 *a young Caesar* — a Roman emperor, and a hero in arms.

18 *the King* — Gustavus Adolphus of Sweden.

18 *Hercules's* — Hercules was a heroic warrior in Greek myth.

19 *The Song of the Girl and the Soldier* — this song fits plausibly into the action as Eilif's party piece, a song and dance as they wait for the cook to bring on the food. Eilif sings the nonchalant verses, and it is left to Courage as the voice of wisdom to sing the last verse with its moral that the wages of bravery are death. The song brings together the group inside and the one outside the tent at the end of the scene. The song derives from Kipling.

19 *bay'nit* — bayonet, a dagger fixed on the end of a long rifle or musket.

19 *wiv' a round up the spout* — loaded, with a bullet in the chamber.

20 *Not surrendering* — Courage is only concerned that Eilif has put his life at risk; his atrocities don't interest her. Eilif doesn't understand. He is temperamentally incapable of keeping his head down and steering clear of trouble.

Scene 3

21 *armourer* — soldier in charge of supplies of weapons and ammunition.

21 *court-martial* — although a civilian, Courage would be dealt with by a military court if she were caught dealing in stolen ammunition.

22 *with your complaint* — Yvette has contracted a venereal disease.

23 *Song of Fraternisation* — the song, though an anti-illusionistic device, fits neatly into the action, being a summary of Yvette's life to date and at the same time a warning to Kattrin not to consort with the soldiery.

25 *pleasing to God* — the Chaplain takes the chance to state the official line on the war. The cook responds with biting sarcasm. The latter's view is close to Courage's but has a total cynicism that she does not possess.

26 *pulling the red boots towards her* — Kattrin's interest in Yvette's hat and boots reveals her frustrated sexuality.

26 *into their own affairs* — Courage is biased. In 'sticking their noses in' the Poles are resisting the invasion of their country by Gustavus Adolphus, King of Sweden. Since the Swedes were Protestants and the Poles Catholics the notion that the Swedish king was doing the Poles a service in liberating them from the Catholic Holy Roman Empire and stripping them of their religion is deeply ironic.

26 *Salt tax* — salt was a state monopoly and carried a tax to pay for the war.

26 *drawn and quartered* — disembowelled and cut in pieces, usually for the parts to be displayed in public places.

27 *emperor* — it was Emperor Ferdinand II who prosecuted the war from Vienna as a crusade to recover for Catholicism lands in North Germany that had been lost to Protestantism. When his soldiers reached the Baltic, and with it the Swedish sphere of influence, Gustavus Adolphus entered the war as champion of Protestantism. The cook counters Courage's biased version of Polish conduct with his own ironic debunking of the Swedish King's heroics in the name of religion.

27 *wouldn't be in it at all* — this is Courage's clearest statement that she, like the war leaders, views the war as a business proposition.

27 *Lutherans* — Protestants.

29 *whore of Babylon* — the abusive term used in the Old Testament for Ishtar, the Babylonian goddess of love and fertility. Courage uses it here to add force to her admonition.

29 *Hide your light under a bushel, it says* — it, namely the Bible, on the contrary says you should *not* hide your light, that is your talents, under a bushel.

30 *Bozhe moi!* — a Polish expletive, 'My God!'

30 *Antichrist* — an abusive, emotive term for the opponent of Christ and his true church. Courage has painted Antichrist as a Protestant devil to curry favour with the Catholic authorities. She views religion as a set of phrases, to be adopted or abandoned as business dictates.

31 *Livonia* — state on the Baltic in the 17th century; capital-Riga (see map). Later it was part of Latvia, and is now in the USSR.

31 *ordinary folk* — Courage has noted (p.27) that in spite of official attitudes the top people are in the war for profit, just as she is. She now observes that top people's victories do not coincide with ordinary people's, and that she has occasionally done better by being on the defeated side.

31 *Lutheran trousers keep out cold too* — this succinct, earthy statement sums up the underlying view that in wartime all trading is fair trading.

32 *mendicant* — mendicant friar, a monk who begs for his living.

32 *like a stone in Dalecarlia* — so ordinary as to merge with the background in that stony province. The image of a stone is taken up on p.80 (see note to p.3).

32 *I'd lief have her* — deliberately archaic phrase meaning I'd prefer her.

34 *All good Catholics here* — the Chaplain, as one would expect, finds it harder to pose as a Catholic than Courage.

34 *heretic* — one who believes in a false faith. Here the position is complicated in that Courage, who has newly adopted the pretence that she is Catholic, is inviting Swiss Cheese who is a Protestant to assure his Catholic captors that he is Catholic.

35 *He ain't all that stupid* — Courage has relied on Swiss Cheese's dull-wittedness and honesty to keep him out of trouble. Now that his honesty (that is, his dedication to duty and the cash-box) looks like being the death of him, quite literally, and Courage hints broadly that the time has come to talk. Swiss Cheese steadfastly refuses to take the hint.

36 *Song of the Hours* — Brecht has adapted a 17th-century religious poem by Christian Weise. Christ and Swiss Cheese are not just two who 'get caught'; they are innocent victims of human malice. In Brecht's production Erwin Geschonneck sang the song quietly and bitterly, as if remembering the days when he was a young clergyman and still believed it was a religious war. It is heartfelt comment on Swiss Cheese's plight, since while remaining detached we still have to believe his death is a real possibility.

40 *an innocent man'll have a chance of being let off* — Courage's ironic view of judicial corruption as the one mitigating factor in the administration of justice reflects Brecht's view that justice is class justice and in an imperfect society will favour the ruling classes. Azdak, the 'good bad judge' in *The Caucasian Chalk Circle* recognises the problem and stands the law on its head to favour the poor.

41 *shove me in a ditch* — Courage's dilemma at this point is that she has to choose between losing her son and losing everything she has built up in thirty years of hard work — she is almost always working when we see her on the stage. Without her waggon the celebrated Mother Courage would be nobody. This is why she is still struggling to salvage something from the situation when the execution is carried out.

42 *Mother Courage remains seated* — this is where Helene Weigel in the Brecht production threw back her head and contorted her face in her famous silent scream of agony.

42 *lansequenets* — mercenary soldiers in 17th-century Germany, from the German 'Landsknecht'.

42 *Mother Courage shakes her head* — the emotional price

Courage pays here for staying in business is high. She only
four laconic words after the death of Swiss Cheese in this s
and her self-control just stretches to the gesture of denial.

Scene 4

43 *Bouque la Madonne!* — a French oath, literally 'kiss the
Madonna!'

44 *corn should be trampled flat* — the tactics Courage describes,
with the wanton destruction of crops after the army had satisfied
its own needs, are historically accurate as well as contributing to
the image which Brecht aims to project of war as a disaster for
civil society.

45 *your anger ain't long enough* — Courage means that it is futile
to give vent to momentary indignation at the injustices of the
system; this implies that a long anger must generate a willingness
to stand up to and even change the system.

45 *Song of the Grand Capitulation* — this song supplies some of
the pre-history of the play, telling us that the young Courage
thought she was somebody special, destined for 'Higher Things'.
In stanza 2 she recollects how quickly her aspirations crumbled
in the face of economic necessity (two kids to feed) and she
found herself marching to 'their tune', a fate, stanza 3 tells us that
befalls all who set out to scale the heights. The song wryly quotes
folk adages for all situations. If 'where there's a will, there's a way'
doesn't work, try 'no good banging your head against a brick wall'.
By the end Courage has persuaded herself as well as the soldier not
to protest. This, in Brecht's own estimate, was her lowest action
in the entire play. (cf. Introduction, p.xxiv)

Scene 5

48 *Tilly's victory at Magdeburg* — Count Johann Tilly (1559-1632),
a key figure in the Thirty Years War, was commander-in-chief of
the Imperial forces from 1630 and led them from victory to
victory until Gustavus Adolphus defeated him at Breitenfeld in
1631. Earlier that year he had sacked Magdeburg in one of the
most vicious engagements of the war. Brecht illustrates the
holocaust by showing a fringe incident.

48 *Town must of paid him* — it is ironic that when the general for
once acts in a humane fashion, the soldier, who feels he has been
deprived of his share of the loot, immediately assumes that the
townspeople have bribed him.

49   *The Chaplain lifts her off the steps* — in the 1941 Zurich version Courage, after some initial grumbles, voluntarily tore up shirts for bandages. The final version makes her less charitable, so as to alienate audience sympathy.

50   *All your victories mean to me is losses* — the war is business by other means, and here Courage is judging it from a personal commercial point of view.

50   *Psia krew!* — Polish oath, 'blood of a dog!'

Scene 6

50   *Tilly* — Tilly was defeated by Gustavus Adolphus at Rain am Lech in 1631 and died later at Ingolstadt of wounds received in the battle.

50   *Kattrin gets the red boots* — Kattrin does not, of course, take the red boots. Brecht's captions are usually explanatory, but this one is cryptic, concealing rather than telling us in advance what happened to Kattrin. When he needs suspense Brecht, in spite of his theories, does not hesitate to use it.

51   *sergeants and up* — sergeants and officers.

52   *them as should be carrying them out* — in this speech Courage recognises that wars cannot be fought without soldiers. A modern audience can draw the conclusion, which would be incredible and anachronistic if Courage were to reach it, that by recognising their class interest and withdrawing their participation the soldiery could stop wars.

53   *emperor and kings and popes* — the essential point about this whimsical speech by the Chaplain on the inevitability and perfectability of war lies in this sentence and its implication. So long as there are emperors, kings and popes . . .

53   *Where is the hole once the cheese has been eaten?* — In this metaphor war is the cheese and peace the hole, so the Chaplain is implying, quite cynically, that war is the natural state of man, and peace does not really exist.

54   *I won* — the clerk and the Chaplain have been playing a board game since the start of the scene.

55   *emperor and pope* — Courage here accurately reviews the lot of the poor and their exploitation by the Church and the aristocracy at this period. She notes that it takes courage to bear it. It is left to the audience to register the need to change it.

55   *Oxenstierna Regiment* — the regiment Eilif joined in scene 1 (see note on p.3). The cook belongs to it too, and the Chaplain is jealous because Courage is smoking the pipe the cook left behind in scene 3. Count Axel Oxenstierna was the Swedish Chancellor.

56 *Don Juans* — womanizers.

56 *Don't chop my chopping block in two* — while warning Courage that the cook is an unscrupulous man of wrath the Chaplain himself wields the axe so violently that he threatens to split the block.

56 *foot-cloth* — strip of cloth wound round the foot instead of a sock. The Chaplain's ability to send men into battle heedless of their lives can be read as an allusion to Hitler's oratory which also conjured up a 'vision of final victory'.

57 *if I'm ruined* — Courage has just made her clearest statement of her aim in life, namely to bring herself and her children through it all with her cart.

58 *before putting them away* — Courage has stored away Yvette's boots after taking them from Kattrin in scene 3 (p.29). For Kattrin they represent sex appeal, so it is singularly clumsy of Courage to offer her them just after she has been attacked and carved up by soldiers. Kattrin leaves them lying (and in Brecht's production Courage stored them away again).

59 *when she was little* — the information that Kattrin's dumbness is traumatic is new. In scene 1 Courage has implied that Kattrin was 'born dumb'.

59 *War be damned* — for a moment Courage learns the true meaning of war.

Scene 7

59 *I won't have you folk spoiling my war for me* — this line was inserted by Brecht in the 1949 production to make the warlike Courage of scene 7 contrast more starkly with the chastened Courage at the end of the previous scene. Courage's business is at its peak as the necklace of silver coins demonstrates. Her song sings the praises of life on the road following the troops, and blithely equates war and business.

Scene 8

60 *Lützen* — small town ten miles west of Leipzig (see map). Gustavus Adolphus defeated the Imperial army under Wallenstein there in 1632, but was killed in action. There is no indication where scene 8 takes place, but it is far enough from Lützen for news of peace to take three weeks to arrive.

62 *parading yourself as a heretic* — since they are still in the Imperial camp the Chaplain would reveal himself as an unbeliever were he to put his Protestant garb back on.

63 *All piss and wind* — a windbag, all talk and no substance.

63 *my good influence* — this must be irony, in view of Yvette's later revelations about the cook.

64 *You are a hyaena of the battlefield* — the Chaplain on war is erratic in his views, talking of a 'war for the faith' in scene 3, proclaiming that there will always be wars, so long as there are emperors, kings and popes in scene 6, then blaming 'those that start wars' for bringing 'humanity's lowest instincts to the surface' at the end of the same scene. If he seems a man of peace here, it is because he is being taunted by Courage and his rival, the cook, because 'his war' has failed to materialize. After this insult he is finished as far as Courage is concerned.

65 *whosoever sups with the devil needs a long spoon* — in a sense Brecht has planted the moral of the play in the Chaplain's lines here as he reiterates in metaphor what the Sergeant in scene 1 stated literally, 'Want to live off the war, but keep your family out of it, eh?' (p.13). This was the warning Brecht's play was supposed to give to Denmark before World War II.

66 *She is much older and fatter* — Yvette has prospered in the war and is now a countess, but she has paid a high price, looking like a fat, powdered old hag though her real age, according to the internal chronology of the play, is only 24. (She sings in the 'Song of Fraternisation' that she was sixteen when she was seduced five years before (cf. p.24). Scene 8 is three years later in 1632.)

68 *'The mills of God grind slowly'* . . . vengeance may be delayed, but will come when least expected. The Chaplain assumes, quite reasonably, that Yvette has put an end to the cook's chances with Courage.

68 *chalky-white* — an alienation effect. As early as *Edward II* (1924) Brecht was using white make-up to show fear, partly on the advice of the Munich comic Karl Valentin.

68 *Provost-marshal* — archaic term for the head of the military police.

70 *I'm joining our side this time* — Courage goes back to the Swedish side again here.

70 *Take more than the war to steal him from me. Clever, he is* — there is dramatic irony here, since the cook has observed that it is precisely for being clever that Eilif is to be shot, and further irony in Courage's formulation, since the 'more than war' which takes

Eilif away is in fact peace.

71 *Where there's smoke there's fire* — a variation of the proverb. 'There's no smoke without fire' which implies that when a person is ill spoken off it cannot be wholly without reason. Courage turns the meaning round to suggest approval of the 'fire', namely the cook's sexual prowess.

71 *The war's still hungry. So enlist!* — this fourth verse of Courage's Song' is the last she sings of her profession and the war with any confidence. In the next scene the play enters its bleak final phase.

Scene 9

72 *Fichtelgebirge* — wooded hills on the border of Germany and Czechoslovakia (see map).

71 *Utrecht* — the cook's native town in Holland (see map).

72 *Saxony . . . Wurttemberg . . . Pomerania* — states in central, south-west and north Germany.

75 *a song concerning Solomon* — Solomon's wisdom, Caesar's bravery, the probity of Socrates and St Martin's charity are all cited as examples of the futility of virtue. It should be noted that bravery and probity have been the undoing both of Eilif — that 'young Caesar' (cf. p.18) — and of 'honest' Swiss Cheese (cf. p.22), and that charity will be the death of Kattrin, just as Courage's own form of wisdom will bring her no satisfaction. The 'Song of Solomon' might have been written as explicit comment on the plot, and yet Brecht had used it earlier, in *The Threepenny Opera*, in praise of immorality in an immoral society. Here the cook sings it to justify his own pragmatism, and it gives Courage time to make up her mind about his offer.

75 *Caesar* — Julius Caesar, Roman general and statesman, assassinated by his friends and colleagues in 45 BC.

76 *poisoned drink* — Socrates, the Greek philosopher, was condemned to death by drinking hemlock.

78 *it ain't you, it's for cart* — Courage has just made what seems like a magnanimous decision to stay with Kattrin, in spite of the song about the dangers of virtue. She now protests that it was a commercial decision and not a maternal one. Does she protest too much?

Scene 10

79 *Courage and Kattrin pause to listen* — the voice sings a folk-song extolling home and garden, domesticity and security. Brecht instructs the actresses in his Model-Book that the vagabond mother and daughter show no emotions here. The audience must imagine what is happening inside them.

Scene 11

80 *Halle* — town in Saxony, frequently ravaged by the Thirty Years War (see map).

80 *The stone begins to speak* — Brecht has prepared us for this metaphor on p.32 where Courage says, 'Let her be like a stone in Dalecarlia, where there's nowt else.' Here Kattrin emerges from her stony inarticulateness to speak through the drum. The ensign (who orders Kattrin to be shot) was played in Brecht's production by the same actor as the young soldier whom Courage prevents from destroying his military career in scene 4.

81 *starving us to death* — we have heard of Eilif's exploits in scene 2 and seen the consequences of the passage of the soldiers in scene 5, but only in this scene does Brecht show them in action, and even here only against the civil population. The peasant's face a similar dilemma to Courage after the arrest of Swiss Cheese, and they too make the economic decision. A life they could spare, but not their livelihood. There would be no life for any of them without their cattle, any more than for Courage's dependents without her waggon.

82 *the eldest's seven* — it is the mention of the children that moves Kattrin to act.

83 *beat the drum* — Kattrin's gesture exposes a hollow passiveness in the peasants' devoutness.

84 *she ain't harmed* — the First Soldier has found the peasants' weak point and naturally assumes he can do the same with Kattrin.

84 *Is nothing sacred to her?* — it is ironic that he should say this of Kattrin, for whom human life, especially where children are concerned, is sacred. For the soldiery who exploit religion, 'sacred' means so close to your own interests that you can be blackmailed through it.

Scene 12

86 *Lullaby baby* — Brecht has adapted a traditional lullaby to fit the situation. Courage still thinks in terms of providing her own children with the best, an echo of her aspirations for herself in the 'Song of the Grand Capitulation'.

87 *Here's money for expenses* — the dramatic situation here is potentially full of pathos. Courage is stricken with grief and unable to grasp at first that Kattrin is dead. To counter this, Courage, in Brecht's production carefully retained one coin as she handed over the contents of her bag to pay for the burial, businesswoman to the last. The later line 'Got to get back into business again' was also a late addition, intended to alienate our sympathies from Courage.

88 *Take me along!* — in spite of all she has lost Courage carries on, without questioning the sense of her way of life. Only a miracle, adds the final verse of 'Courage's Song', can save the common man. Or is there another way? The play is open-ended and leaves the audience facing a question mark.

Scene 1. *Above*: the first sight of the cart and Courage and her family (p.4). *Below:* the Recruiter leads Eilif away (*right*) while Courage haggles (*left*) (p.12). *Photos: Ruth Berlau*

Above: Eilif (*centre*) dances with his sabre (p.19). *Below:* Kattrin (*left*) sees the soldiers come to arrest Swiss Cheese (*right*) (p.33). *Photos: Percy Paukschta*

The closing moments of Scene 3: (*above*) Courage is confronted with Swiss Cheese's body but (*below*) refuses to recognise it. *Photos: Berlau*

Above: Courage sings the Song of the Grand Capitulation (p.46).
Photo: Berlau. Below: Kattrin raises a plank and threatens Courage
with it (p.49). *Photo: Paukschta*

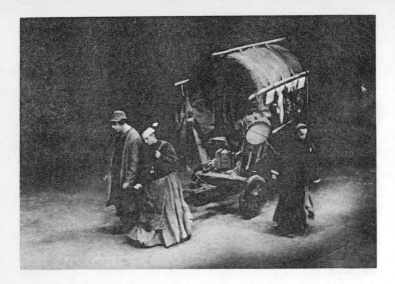

Above: Courage 'at the peak of her business career' — the Chaplain and Kattrin pull the cart (p.59). *Photo: Berlau. Below:* Eilif (*right*) under arrest (p.68). *Photo: Paukschta*

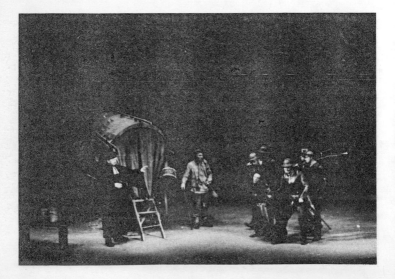

Above: Courage and the cook sing the Song of Solomon (p.75).
Photo: Paukschta. Below: Kattrin, on the roof, is shot (p.86).
Photo: Berlau

Scene 12. *Above:* Courage with the dead Kattrin (p.86).
Below: the end of the play (p.87). *Photos: Berlau*